ENGLISH | SPANISH

JIGS & LURES

Selected Poems || REINA MARÍA RODRÍGUEZ

Foreword and English translations
by KRISTIN DYKSTRA

𝒜
'Alliteration

JIGS AND LURES: SELECTED POEMS | REINA MARÍA RODRÍGUEZ
Translated from the Spanish by Kristin Dykstra
First edition in English in October 2024

© Reina María Rodríguez
© Foreword and English translations by Kristin Dykstra
© Alliteration Publishing, 2024

www.thealliteration.us

Design by Elena Roosen
Cover by Andrea Martínez
Proofreading by Tess Rankin & Félix García
Editorial Coordination by Amayra Velón

ISBN: 979-8-9909355-4-9

HEAT LIGHTNING

I. INTRODUCING THIS EDITION

Reina María Rodríguez is known for her ability to temper light with shadow, drawing haunting images out of the bright everyday streets of Havana. *Jigs and Lures* collects a set of her interlocking poems from the early 2000s that showcase an important stage of the writer's career.

This was a time when Rodríguez grew and changed as a writer, even though she had already produced mature writing. She was confronting the long-term results of social crisis, while seeking new directions and aesthetic possibilities. She examined the city around her, the seawaters near which she has lived her entire life, the sky above them.

These three collections demonstrate her diverse artistic responses to a broader backdrop: the prolongation of Cuba's Special Period in a Time of Peace across decades. The phrase is a euphemism used on the island to name a period of response to severe economic fallout from global realignments after 1989. Though the Special Period specifically connotes the 1990s, impacts from that decade extended into the twenty-first century, with profound effects on islanders.

For this bilingual selection, we include the majority of the poems from Rodríguez's collection *Catch and Release* (2006), pairing them with selections from other books. The artistic

3

continuities and contrasts are revealing of her poetics and their time: poems we selected from *El libro de las clientas* (*The Book of Clients*) and *Bosque negro* (*Black Forest*) coincided, in their general period of composition, with those of *Catch and Release*.[1]

In this commentary, I'll say more about each of those three collections. I'll also include a short overview in section II, situating Rodríguez and this moment within her larger writing career. Her international renown as a writer in the Spanish language has not yet been met with the level of commentary it deserves, particularly for readers of English. It's a pattern all too common with Latin American women's writing to date, even though there are excellent writers and scholars working to redress that imbalance.

If the context in section II is not of interest to you, then by all means, skip it and go on to read sections on the individual books. Yet I suggest keeping this arc in mind: Rodríguez has long dedicated herself to finding ways to carve a literary, humanizing space out of highly polarized and often discouraging contexts. She is known as someone who has insisted on keeping creative community alive and expanding independent spaces for the arts in civil society. This determination has lifted all of her own work to new places.

As this translation moves to publication in the US, it has become common to talk about perceptions that our society is becoming ever more polarized, even as daunting challenges (such as the need to combat climate change) demand that we work together. We too struggle with ways to feel part of a larger community at a time of urgent personal and social need, and many of us talk about why the arts matter despite all discouragements and losses. We struggle to see how language could provide alternatives to the use of force and lead toward resolution of conflict, and —perhaps directly related—we consider how the arts examine our own uncertainties and internal conflicts. To me, these conversations lend extra interest to a writer like Rodríguez, who shares—and writes through—her struggles to address society with honesty, care, and the openness to complexity that the arts can enable. I therefore have included this condensed background on Rodríguez and her very interesting generation.

The context in section II also addresses one of the careless phrases in English-language publishing. Cuban life did not *literally* freeze in 1959, despite our media's insistence upon that idea.

Stray images passed down from the Cold War don't allow us to grasp much about the beauty and struggle of literary Cuba in our own time. So much has happened since 1959—entire literary lifetimes! They are too compelling to ignore.

So too is the fact that we live in a time of diasporas, including a large and diverse US-based Cuban diaspora that now enfolds Reina María Rodríguez herself.

II. AESTHETIC IDENTITIES, GENERATIONALLY
SPEAKING

Critics have long found it challenging to summarize the full range of Rodríguez's aesthetic production. She took inspiration from both colloquial and confessional modes in Latin American poetry from the 1980s forward, yet no one finds these terms adequate for encapsulating her career.

By the time Rodríguez wrote *Catch and Release*, *El libro de las clientas*, and *Bosque negro*, she was already established in both national and international circles. With the benefit of hindsight, we can see that her evolution was by no means finished, so these three books represent a step toward her later works.

A common starting point for poetry analysis in Latin America is to consider poets within a generational movement, which can be useful—up to a point—with these poems in *Jigs and Lures*. The disclaimer is necessary because generational frames divert our attention from individuality and the details that make particular literary works successful. As a starting point, though, they allow readers of translation to take in unfamiliar but essential sociohistorical context.

Rodríguez was a very young child when the 1959 Revolution took place, publishing her first poems in the 1970s. Critics tend to associate her with the poetic Generation of the '80s, or the first group of poets to be fully formed under the post-1959 social order. Cuban revolutionary rhetoric particularly idealized a "New Man" when envisioning the generations to come.

For Jorge Cabezas Miranda, author of an impressive study on late-twentieth-century Cuban poetry, situating Rodríguez as a "precursor" to Cuba's '80s generation is an important step.[2] Most of them are a bit younger than Rodríguez and had formative experiences of Cuban life at a somewhat different moment, context that ties into the reason one uses a generational structure at all, especially around the symbolically loaded moment of 1959. Yet Cabezas also goes on to complicate his own proposal of Rodríguez being a "precursor," describing her as "particularly involved with younger creators."[3]

That ongoing involvement was well symbolized in the 1990s by her use of her rooftop home in Havana as a cultural salon, known as the Azotea (rooftop), hosting readings in a space that is both communitarian and located outside the formal bounds of the state.[4] In our conversations, Rodríguez has always emphasized the importance of setting age aside to listen for artistic affinities, a key element of her vision for energizing and reenergizing creativity.

It's generally agreed that Rodríguez shares the '80s generation's interest in complicating populist attention to community identity and public expression (influential artistic goals within revolutionary Cuba in earlier decades). Also generally noted is her recuperation of value for private dimensions of life and language, an aesthetic trait she shares with the somewhat younger writers.

These correspondences fit into a larger pattern linking Rodríguez, the '80s poets, and island society. Osmar Sánchez Aguilera observes that the '80s generation expresses values corresponding to wider trends in the decade used to name them within Cuban culture: "Tolerance toward positions not shared by all, acceptance of diversity in a growing number of respects, preference for dialogue instead of belligerence in interpersonal relations as well as political relations, a spirit restoring value to individuality, and the consequent right to a comprehensive personhood are some of those values."[5]

Beyond such generalizations, Rodríguez and this cohort of poets can be difficult to describe in brief. Valuing complexity and range, they took on a wide range of subjects and experimented with many forms, as well as reflecting an increasing social diversity among writers (i.e., in contrast to the heavily male, light-skinned, and publicly heterosexual figures who rose to prominence in the 1960s).[6]

Even decades later, commentators have asserted that poetic legacies from the '80s (not to mention works created by these same writers in subsequent decades) have yet to see much treatment from literary critics and scholars. The lack of extended commentary is due in part to the economic crisis that crippled the publishing industry and other Cuban institutions in the 1990s.[7] Paper shortages prevented both commentary and literary works from going to press for years, muddying periodization and analysis. One can only speculate about the amount of literature, local commentary, and criticism that might have been composed and published under less grueling circumstances—a relatively abstract aspect of sociopolitical crisis, yet one with enormous impact for the afterlife of cultural works.

The aesthetic strategies that Rodríguez weaves into the poems gathered here bridge her major works from the 1990s into more recent decades. Her collection *La foto del invernadero* (*The Winter Garden Photograph*) appeared in 1998. Responding to the writer's sense of ideological exhaustion at the close of the twentieth century, the layered poems in that book meld her long-term dedication to Havana as a creative city-space with her ongoing drive to split reality open, writing from a "falla del tiempo" ("a fault line in time").[8]

7

Otras cartas a Milena (*Other Letters to Milena*), dedicated to her youngest child, the daughter that Rodríguez was raising amid crisis, is an inter-genre work also set in Havana, melding poetry with prose. It delves into psychological and aesthetic experiences of disaster and was eventually published in 2003 (with a bilingual edition dating to 2014). *Otras cartas a Milena* prefigures her explorations of how crisis sets local communities into diasporic motion.

In both of those collections, Rodríguez balances an intense commitment to her local time and place against equally consistent and opposing movement, effectively seeking to create a new space among polarities. *Here* coexists with *there*, *place* with *nonplace*; and creativity operates at the junctures of these oppositions.

III. ABOUT *CATCH AND RELEASE*

At the heart of this edition are poems from the prizewinning collection *Catch and Release* (2006). Rodríguez opens by presenting the writer herself as a character, demonstrating a new iteration of distance from herself. In its first text, Rodríguez outlines "the cutout doll of a writer, a character (not skeletal or sentimental or radical or committed)."

By explicitly discarding those descriptions, each associated with earlier images and idealizations of writers, Rodríguez asserts an aesthetic identity for her writer doll only in the duration of her search for an intangible future: creative endurance is itself the wellspring of survival.

As *Catch and Release* unfolds, Rodríguez asserts the essential nature of the arts as tools for survival by tracing the desires of poets, novelists, actors, dancers, musicians, painters, and film viewers. Her serial protagonists encounter limitations that they may choose to confront but rarely surpass. As the possibilities of art meet conditions of human impossibility, poetry generously arranges for the existence of other worlds.

Rodríguez gave her original work the title of *Catch and Release*—already in English—setting up fishing as a metaphor for daily creation. A key poem centers on fishermen who "haul out something changeable, / the fishermen riding the wall like horsemen." The book title suggests that their actions, the catch and release, are more essential than whatever is caught. It hints that the gestures and figures of creators will be significant throughout the book.

The poem "Jigs and Lures," like the scenes traced with light in the introductory text, acts as a more global touchstone for this entire edition. It too has an English-language title referencing fishing, but its contents depart from the literal descriptions we might expect. Here Rodríguez hooks readers by setting her mother's figure into a slow-motion circuit through the plays of light and dark comprising their home, which she also describes as a tapestry. The poem's transgressive, prose-like bulk embodies the writer's desire to meld everyday life and family memories with places only she can create. Nearly every poem that follows can be opened like a Russian doll, disclosing elements of distinct scope.

Rodríguez began her composition of *Catch and Release* with a focus on "the filings of the self," a detail confided in the epigraph to the title poem for that book. She chose details from everyday life, particularly its difficulties, to explore from new angles—a pattern that continues in all of the poems we selected for this edition, even as her central subject matter shifts. A particularly intense curiosity about the daily meanings of loss and mortality threads through all three books, triggered by past events that include the sudden passing of the author's father during her adolescence, then her brother's eventual suicide.

The poems represent Rodríguez well in their ongoing links to her home, family, memories, and key patterns in her literary career. But do not seek documentary here. Mirrored, full of crosscuts, many poems yield interior views intersecting with other people, other writers, other times and places. Continuing the pattern from her major writings of the 1990s, Rodríguez creates a counterpoint between the intense commitment to her local time and place and an equally consistent and opposing movement outwards.

A lyric subject exists in these poems, yet it is broken and multiplied, personal and intertextual, sometimes driven to the cusp of abstraction. The self is elusive, escaping ideological demands, determined to set its own course. The subject's commitment to motion introduces a risk of splitting into uncontrollable mirror selves and simulacra. Threats then arise from other zones. One threat involves losses of memory and connection. Another is the ungraspable future absence demarcated by death. Can the writer find any way to hold a life together, to grasp its significance in the face of fragmentation?

Rodríguez blurs her personal experience into the broadest planes of social experience. In *Catch and Release*, for example, a building that collapses in "I don't hear, don't hear Bach anywhere…" offers a metaphor for hardship and transformation in Cuba's capital city. Other subtle emphases on shortage, disorientation, and creativity are similarly relevant to the difficulties and needs of her historical moment. Rodríguez herself sees a thorough problematization of desire and faith as a characteristic of her writing from this time.

Catch and Release reveals frequent references to objects that fall short of desires, a conscious gesture that she uses to indicate everyday experiences of economic and social limitation. The opening text, a short prose block that refers to a tabletop made of plastic rather than glass, flags this recurrent theme. Rodríguez told me that this text, for her, is about a world cobbled together out of its own unrealities. There everything is a substitute for something else that seems more substantial and more "real": it is a cue to see her contemporary world in terms of pastiche and kitsch.

A different dimension of social involvement in the poems we selected for this bilingual edition involves literary society, generated in her mirrored worlds on the page. One of her strategies for creating a signature intellectual and artistic depth involves a commitment to the constant (re-)creation of artistic community with both the living and the dead. Contemporary writers appear here, some as the dedicatees of poems and others transformed into symbols. There is a splintered dialogue about contemporary Cuban life, which Rodríguez evokes with her friends and fellow writers.

Not to be overlooked is a series of deceased authors from other nations, whom Rodríguez places on an unresolved boundary between individual consciousness and the depersonalizing force of rhetorical figuration, or antonomasia: in death and text, individual authors move toward the (dangerously?) abstract state of poet-as-symbol. The final poem from *Catch and Release* refers to the death of Virginia Woolf, whose prose has long inspired Rodríguez. Marina Tsvetaeva and Anna Akhmatova shimmer at the surface of scattered poems, belying assumptions that Russian cultural influences have evaporated into the clouds in Cuba's post–Cold War era. Samuel Beckett makes another of his various appearances in her writing. Readers interested in intertextuality can thus find numerous prompts here, serving the poet's dynamic oppositions between here and there, then and now.

IV. ABOUT *THE BOOK OF CLIENTS*

During the same period when she was composing *Catch and Release*—from the late 1990s into the early 2000s—Rodríguez developed poems for *The Book of Clients*. In this collection, she dedicates extended reflection to her mother's labor as a seamstress, as well as the impacts of her father's infidelities and early death on the family.

To gain a new perspective on poetic language as a material, Rodríguez trained her attention on delicate and slippery textures, comparable to the fabrics that her mother had to manage while creating clothes. These poems demonstrate her ability to take literal, everyday details of women's work and place them into forms enabling unsettling proposals about larger themes like trust and distrust, life and death.

Poems such as "Threads," "Counted threads," and "Mist in the capital city" exemplify her handling of those themes. "Ignorant women" similarly repurposes a domestic landscape, this time inspired by life elsewhere, referring to the tragic deaths of four women and the backdrop of their home under the high ridgelines of the Chilean cordillera. "Céline and the women" is another major poem from *The Book of Clients*, merging the fabrication of lace with pointed queries about the fabric of familial relationships and the ongoing problem of trust.

During a 2013 reading by Rodríguez in Dallas, the Cuban writer and critic Francisco Morán listened to her read "Céline and the women." Morán (who previously lived in Havana and participated in literary events hosted by Rodríguez) then speculated that her daily fabrication of literature recreates a childhood immersion in her mother's everyday workspace. Rodríguez liked Morán's way of situating her literary identity.

When Rodríguez received the prestigious Pablo Neruda Ibero-American Poetry Award in Chile in 2014, one of her first public reactions was to describe herself as the daughter of a seamstress. That connection probably says something not only about her own commitment to writing as everyday labor, but about why so many audiences find Rodríguez and her writing approachable despite their sophistication.

Accompanying her daily construction of poetry is another long-term characteristic through which Rodríguez rises above the fray. This is the rigorous, occasionally merciless intellectual undercurrent that propels each of her books. Insofar as *Catch and Release* is "about" mortality and poetry, or the limitations faced by artists hoping to create new worlds, literal deaths merge with metaphorical death to travel across the scene of writing, invading every layer of the work. *The Book of Clients* addresses mortality by way of images such as the fraying edges of a cloth—marking a point of limitation, beyond which all humanity falls apart.

V. ABOUT *BLACK FOREST*

The third collection represented within this edition again approaches human mortality—but now with a unique and more gritty artistic strategy. What becomes more explicit via the dry clarities of *Black Forest* is the sociopolitical atmosphere of shortage and anxiety lingering into the new century. Despite the fact that its creation overlaps with those of the other works, this book is formally distinct. Rodríguez carries out more extensive mixing of end-stopped lines with blocks of prose poetry. But it is in tone that these poems stand out the most: in the opening poem of *Black Forest*, she emphasizes the "dry" and "lucid" voice she crafted for this collection addressing crisis, in implicit contrast to the liquid, slippery tones of the others.

That poem, "See if it arrived...," addresses a fellow poet, Ismael González Castañer. He participated in the informal cultural salon that Rodríguez ran out of her home in the 1990s, the Azotea. González wrote a poem about the turmoil of the Special Period called "Vacaciones en el mundo" ("A Vacation in the World"), a phrase that Rodríguez repeats.[9] His satirical poem presents contrasts between past and present, such as a declaration of personal conviction turned on its head: "I was fat / and now there's proof / that skinny is better." This mini-revolution of ideas, not coincidentally invoking the hunger of the Special Period, is followed by a judgment about a communal "we": "We were confused in the world / our existence due more than anything to a very good lubricant" (in context, apparently referring to a petroleum-based lubricant for machines).

Rodríguez recalls that the very idea of traveling outside the island was impossible for most people, given widespread economic limitations. She also recalls her feeling that citizens were watching their expectations for their own lives fail amid a drastic diminution of possibilities, a sensation bridging his poem to her response. González Castañer highlights the point that vacations in the world beyond the island were not within reach. In her response, Rodríguez drops his use of ironic humor—she often remarks that humor isn't part of her range as a poet—but keeps his emphasis on the historic levels of disruption.

Rodríguez situates her own voice as emerging from the far side of writing. In the poetic search for her composition notebook, she suggests a quest for demythologization, moving toward a new ground that she does not yet seem to have discovered, despite her realization that the old ground has fallen away. *Black Forest* introduces a new focus on basic daily needs—cooking oil, detergent, food. As she states in "Oils," she also needs a lubricant, turning the petroleum product from González Castañer's poem into a sexual product, but then she lacks the courage to request it from a store in Miami Beach.

A poem she has often chosen to read in live events, "Fricandeau," resulted from a real conversation with the poet Almelio Calderón. He came to her rooftop to talk about poetry, bearing a strange new food. Calderón told Rodríguez that his family had substituted pickled grapefruit for steak, because protein was especially hard to obtain. Decades later, Rodríguez still retells this story with a tone of amazement, suggesting a moment she struggles to fully apprehend.

Poems from *Black Forest* voice the awareness that with options for writers and artists drying up on the island, emigration had begun to alter the face of the creative community. The rise of migration as a theme links Rodríguez's Cuba to many other societies that have become "sending countries" in the twenty-first century. For example, Almelio Calderón now lives in Spain. The clipped prose of "Voices" dramatizes the multiplication of these absences, distances the poet struggles to cross by telephone. To the oppositions of here and there, then and now, we can add another creative opposition expressing realities of diaspora: *present/absent*.

Once we recognize the centrality of emigration and diaspora to *Black Forest*, it is possible to circle back into *Catch and Release*, which foreshadowed the importance of this theme within its own, more liquid registers. "The classroom turtle" hints at the importance of emigration to more than one generation. *Catch and Release* also includes an exemplary poem blending the dream of artistic community with the problem of emigration: "The word *pitcher*."

Many years ago, Rodríguez told me that the figure of the poet in this text is loosely based on Javier Marimón, a younger writer who participated in readings she organized in the 1990s, and who occasionally typed his writing on her computer, since he didn't have one of his own. The poem emerges from his physical presence and the implicit interest of their conversations, but even more from basic practicalities of getting literature made in Havana during times of crisis.

By the time we discussed this poem, crisis had precipitated his departure from the Havana cultural scene. Marimón lives outside the island, in Puerto Rico—not far from Cuba in geographical terms but not available for artistic conversation—so in her book, his image becomes another iteration of absence in Cuban literary community. Embedded distance is the new reality of "local" life in Havana in the twenty-first century, something that migrants from many other nations may also recognize given the global importance of emigration and diaspora in this century.

VI. AT LAST THE REASON THIS ESSAY IS CALLED
"HEAT LIGHTNING"
As many readers who experienced the global COVID-19 pandemic may themselves understand today, crises give rise to both exhaustion and creativity. When crises extend across years, across entire families, societies, and regions, they are life-altering for those who endure. They alter the fabric of the realities in which we live.

Amid all the noise accompanying a new century, Rodríguez was seeking the daily contours of emergency, in which boundaries and limitations on human desires remained present. Hers is a poetics of care for an exhausted humanity. We can also see in her complex body of work myriad ways of turning writing into a daily expression of human resourcefulness and power. Reina María Rodríguez illustrates how patience at one's work yields a continuously renewed sense of purpose, curiosity, the will to endure, and an ability to convert everyday conditions into poetry.

Above all, she shows us how to generate energy from our own actions. Her most committed, daily acts of creation parallel those of her fishermen at their labors: to catch up images in her poems, then release them back to the life flowing around her. The flickering of heat lightning is our warning and our reward.

VII. REGARDING THE TRANSLATION

For this translation I've undertaken a layered process influenced by various sources, including my readings of other literary translations and poetry important to Rodríguez. She has been generous about making time in her demanding schedule to review details. Over the years I've found that our conversations help me to discover new ways to render her wording.

Her poetry frequently includes very specific reference points yet is calibrated with ambiguous and elusive phrases. The translator too must enact creative oppositions in language, between *here* and *there*, *then* and *now*, *present* and *absent*.

This discussion process is more complex than it sounds. My conversations with Rodríguez bring me "closer" to her poems on some level, but my translations blend this familiarity with degrees of intuition and resistance. This is because her poetics turns on the impossible capture of distance. It is imperative that the translator not try to rewrite her delicate phrasing as though the poetry were straightforward documentation, anchored in one predictable place.

"Story" and "history" are present but ruptured. Put differently, the poetry is about the disruption and estrangement of daily life. This process operates in a register generated by someone whose daily life is very much of the mind as well as the body.

16

In order to capture the moments that did need to be concrete or anchored in a particular way within the overall balance of each poem, we discussed backstories that allow me to identify subjects as needed in the English translation (*he* vs. *she* or *it*, which can often be blurred in the Spanish). Rodríguez clarified many other contextual facets, showing me family photographs and walking me around places related to individual poems, telling me the stories they recalled. Yet because each poetic catch is paired with a release, I apply that knowledge with restraint.

To the oppositions noted above, I would add *self* and *other*. Of course, this opposition sits at the heart of literary translation. However, it acquires extra registers when one does multiple projects with a writer like Rodríguez, who has been making self *other* in all of her mature works, including every book I previously translated by her. As a result, a literary performance of her writing in English requires the translator to also make self *other*, operating outside of one's own element.

The phrases "the poet's language" and "the translator's language" offer a straightforward parallel equation used in discussion of translations. While practical, and perhaps inescapable, this framework is inadequate for talking about *what it actually feels like* to work in especially dynamic aesthetic zones. Rodríguez does tap into a legacy of colloquialism in post-1959 Cuban poetry, but she also goes beyond everyday or conversational expression in her continual search for aesthetic resources, so translation should too. I offer this translation as a negotiation among "the poet's languages and her not-languages" as well as "the translator's language and her not-languages."

Kristin Dykstra

NOTES

1   The title of the book, *Bosque negro*, was later reused as the title of an anthology. Here I refer to the original poetry collection.

2   Jorge Cabezas Miranda, *Proyectos poéticos en Cuba, 1959–2000: Algunos cambios formales y temáticos* (Alicante: Publicaciones de la Universidad de Alicante, 2012), 154.

3   Cabezas Miranda, *Proyectos poéticos*, 193. Unless otherwise noted, translations are my own.

4   Various extended discussions of the Azotea now appear in English. See the prologue and interview in *The Winter Garden Photograph* (New York: Ugly Duckling Presse, 2019). The digital magazine *Latin American Literature Today* later published essays in a bilingual dossier dedicated to Rodríguez in 2021, including updates regarding the role of the rooftop home in her overall career. See "Featured Author: Reina María Rodríguez," dossier, *Latin American Literature Today* 18 (May 2021), archived online at https://latinamericanliteraturetoday.org/section/featured-author-reina-maria-rodriguez/
    Of particular relevance within that magazine dossier is "After the Azotea" ("Más allá de la Azotea"), by Elena Lahr-Vivaz. In 2022, Lahr-Vivaz published a scholarly book, *Writing Islands: Space and Identity in the Transnational Cuban Archipelago* (Gainesville: University of Florida Press, 2022). In chapter 2, "Birds of a Feather," she provides a meticulous discussion that places Rodríguez and the Azotea in the context of a larger, transnational Cuban cultural archipelago.

5   Osmar Sánchez Aguilera, "Poesía en claro. Cuba, años 80 (Long play/variaciones)," *Revista del Ateneo Puertorriqueño* 2, no. 5 (1992): 67–87, 70 See also a chapter in which I give a broader range of comments on generational and historical contexts involving poetry from 1959 to 1989: Kristin Dykstra, "Cuba's Poetic Imaginary (1959-1989)," in *The Cambridge History of Cuban Literature*, edited by Vicky Unruh and Jacqueline Loss (Cambridge UP, 2024), pp. 438-453.

6   Isabel Alfonso discusses the suppression of a more diverse group of poets with the closing of Ediciones El Puente, in "Radical Poetics of the Sixties in Cuba: The Case of Ediciones El Puente and Its Revolutionary Existentialism," trans. Sue Ashdown, *Public* 26, no. 52 (2015): 203–219. Amina Damerdji traces patterns of gender and sexuality around the creation of *El caimán barbudo* in "Commitment Trouble: Gender Performances and Poetic Dissent in the Cuban Revolution," *Latin American Literary Review* 45, no. 90 (2018): 44–52.

7   See for example Norge Espinosa's observations in "Poesía cubana / años ochenta / un vacío en el espejo de la crítica," *Aula Lírica* 8 (2016): 30–36.

8   From the poem, "El frío" ("The cold"). The complete poem appears in both languages on pages 46–47 of the 2019 bilingual edition from Ugly Duckling Presse.

9   In a telephone conversation with me, Rodríguez recalled details about her poem as an intentional dialogue with González Castañer (July 26, 2021). An English translation of his complete poem by Todd Ramón Ochoa, from which these translated phrases are taken, appears in *The Whole Island: Six Decades of Cuban Poetry, A Bilingual Anthology*, ed. Mark Weiss (Berkeley: The University of California Press, 2009).

JiGS & LURES

ENGLISH | SPANISH

CATCH AND RELEASE
CATCH AND RELEASE
(2006)

Así que yo también entraba en un bosque

Así que yo también entraba a un bosque —simulado por la buganvilia sembrada muchos años atrás en un cantero de metal. Más allá, la mesa blanca redondeaba mi ambición de ver aún los destellos de una mañana más. Las casas pintarrajeadas, los hierros retorcidos de la infancia, los sonidos vulgares de la necesidad que se fundían cercanos (en mi visión) al paisaje de la desolación real que era, por aquellos tiempos, mi vida. Los mismos flacos pájaros, el gato envejecido sobre un raído cojín, con sus líneas pintadas por la luz en la calcomanía, perseguía con los ojos vendados una paloma roja que nunca se atrevió a comer, y un "lo mismo tal vez..." de aquel vuelo mantenido como espejo, como coreografía. Por este camino hacia el bosque mañanero —hacia mi vejez—, hacia el personaje recortado de una escritora (ni huesuda ni sentimental ni radical ni comprometida) siempre esperando que la suerte —como un viejo amor inconforme— llegara a sorprenderla con un toque de queda en redondo a la puerta —igual al sonido de aquella mesa plástica por cristal—, cuyos peces soñaba que cogía y soltaba por el imaginario roto cada día, y le trajera (y me dejara), "aquello" perdido para siempre que el verano le negó.

So I would go into a forest too

So I would go into a forest too—one simulated by the bougainvillea planted many years ago inside a metal garden frame. Behind it the white table, which curved my determination to spot the glints given off by one more morning. Colorwashed houses, twisted railings from my childhood, vulgar sounds of need that merged nearby (inside my vision) into the landscape of real devastation then constituting my life. The same skinny birds, a cat aging on a threadbare cushion, their patterns traced by the light passing through paper, simulating a stained-glass window; wearing an eyepatch, the cat would track a red dove, never daring to eat it, and a "maybe same thing..." from the bird's flight sustained as mirror, as choreography. Down this road toward the dawning forest—toward my old age—toward the cutout doll of a writer, a character (not skeletal or sentimental or radical or committed) always hoping for fate—like a nonconformist love from the past—to arrive and surprise her with a curfew just around the other side of the door—the same sound made by the table constructed with plastic instead of glass. She dreamt every day about catching fish in her torn imaginary and then releasing them. It would bring her (and leave me) the perpetually lost "thing" that summer denied.

No oigo, no oigo a Bach por ninguna parte...

...mientras la señorita tocaba
el último acorde de la fuga de Bach...

Las fusas, "esas garrapatas dobles sobre el pentagrama"
—las llamaba Fe—, con la gravedad
que tanto trabajo costaba interpretar.
La intensidad perdida de aquellas semifusas
con insatisfacciones.
Cantatas sacras de un subterfugio cualquiera
y salir brincando por la ventana del baño
hacia la mañana de un domingo lluvioso
(el piano encerrado todavía dentro de la casa)
enloquecido por los arrebatos de Melchor
sobre sus cuerdas rotas,
en un vulgar programa de música clásica por la radio
donde una mano cualquiera
lo golpea indiferente hoy.
Y ella buscando atrás, atrás,
una fuga sin terminar,
ciento veintinueve compases que simbolizan
la palabra obsesión, y luego
el llanto.

Ya no oigo a Bach por ninguna parte
en la versión de Wanda Landowskca.
No oigo sus tropeles (esos devaneos),
sus cizañas.
De manera que a mi sensibilidad
la corrompió también esas esquirlas
que sin querer nos sobrepasan.
Todo mi dinero invertido en comprar aquellos discos

I don't hear, don't hear Bach anywhere...

*...as Miss Craye struck
the final chord of the Bach fugue...*

Thirty-second notes, "those double ticks over the staff"
—as Faith called them—with the gravity
that took so much work to perform.
Lost intensity of those sixty-fourth notes,
restless.
Religious cantatas for a prosaic escape
and leaping out the bathroom window in a rush
toward a rainy Sunday morning
(piano still shut inside the house)
maddened by Melchor's paroxysms
over its broken strings,
on a radio program of classical music, lacking in taste:
today someone's hand
bangs at the piano indifferently.
And behind her, behind her, the woman searching,
a never-ending fugue,
one hundred twenty-nine measures to symbolize
the word obsession, and then
weeping.

Now I don't hear Bach anywhere
in Wanda Landowska's rendition.
I no longer hear her medleys (those flings),
her discords.
Such that my sensibility
was also corrupted, those splinters
overwhelming us.
All my money invested in buying those records,

27

gradualmente sonándoles más la inconformidad
—menos la devoción cada vez—
tras un deseo ingrato por las cosas
que no vienen rayadas en la placa.
Oírte regresar por la escalera del arpegio
con futilidad, con desdén.
Ruidos, atropellos, sarcasmos...
(Contrabando en La Casa de la Cultura Checa,
que tampoco existe ya, en Py 23.)

Iba a los conciertos los domingos
con aquel vestidito de seda gris
y el hueco es cada vez más profundo, más repugnante,
entre aquella muchacha sencilla
y yo.
Será que anduve de viaje por la inutilidad
de un sentir?
Será que el teatro se quemó bajo una cúspide de resonancia
frágil?

La casa se derrumbó una mañana de domingo
hacia la esquina de Neptuno,
y las teclas sonaron sin Fe
sobre mi espalda abotonada al nácar de un teclado
que había dado la vuelta (en redondo) al mundo de una esquina,
sobre amarillos arrancados de cuajo
—a una tecla, a un botón, a las aproximaciones
de mis manos—
con esa pobre indiferencia de las muchachas
comprometidas con nada
(pero con algo aprendido de aquella vanidad pecaminosa)
sospechando que valdría muy poco sostener
aquel sí definitivo.
"¿Para quién?" —me preguntaba Fe desde el teclado.

nonconformity sounding more and more clearly
—devotion less and less—
because of an ungrateful desire for things
that don't come etched into the surface.
Hearing you return along the arpeggio's steps
with futility, with disdain.
Noise, bursts of outrage, sarcastic remarks…
(Contraband in the House of Czech Culture
at the corner of P and 23rd, which no longer exists either.)

I used to go to concerts on Sundays
in a little gray silk dress
the gap grows ever deeper, more repugnant,
between that simple girl
and me.
Was I traveling through some sterilized
sensation?
Did the theater burn below its peak
of fragile resonance?

The house fell down one Sunday morning
on the corner at Neptune,
and the keys rang out without Faith,
over my back, buttoned with mother-of-pearl from a keyboard
that revolved (all the way around) through the world of a street
corner,
over yellows plucked in clots
—from a key, a button, the approximations
of my hands—
with that poor indifference of girls
engaged to nothing
(but with something learned from sinful vanity)
suspecting it would be worth very little to maintain
the definitive yes.
"For whom?" Faith would ask me from her keyboard.

Fue mi pasión, lo sé, trucar los dedos
de un semitono, equívoco.

En fin, no me quejo.
Pero queda esa confusión, esa desazón,
esa vaga nostalgia que se llamaba música
contra los pedales al chocar
muy des-pa-cio primero
(aprisa luego),
con arrepentimiento
de bronce mal pulido bajo la piel,
corrompiéndose allí
(reverberando)
en el dorado champagne de otras imágenes
pasadas por los dedos.
"¡Un delirio mal tocado!" —gritaba ella—,
un dolor de las fusas clavadas en el pecho,
a contrapunto, alta traición
de un tiempo desmedido,
pero "absolutamente medido"
—decía muy segura—
entre un compás y otro,
contra el miedo.

It was my passion, I know, setting my fingers
for a half note. Ambiguous.

Well, I'm not complaining.
But the confusion remains, unease,
vague nostalgia named as music
clashing against the pedals
ve - - ry slow - - ly
(then in a rush),
remorse
from badly polished bronze, there under the skin,
stagnating
(reverberating)
in the golden champagne of other images
passing under my fingers.
"A badly executed delirium!"—she cried,
pain from thirty-second notes pounded into my chest,
counterpoint, high treason
of an immoderate tempo,
but "absolutely measured"
—she said with great certainty—
between one bar and another,
measured off against the fear.

Jigs and Lures

El cielo inmenso que me pertenece ha caído en un detalle de mi plegaria. Yo lo creía cambiar desde los amarillos, a los fuegos intensos. Él mentía. Era mi visión la que cambiaba de ángulo. Lo demás pasará. La pasión, la vida, la necesidad de ser abrazada, el don. Toda esta inútil persecución de la nada cuando una nube está a punto de cambiar su rumbo y disolverla. Él quedaría allí, fijo en sus circunvalaciones, con sus metáforas, con su luz —la que aún yo pueda ver. Las grietas del muro y el relámpago de calor logran el juego por todo lo que falta en esta tarde y ella, mi madre, como una sonámbula, también camina ahora por toda la casa que es redonda y circular como un pequeño tapiz. Creo que ya tendré otra fórmula de concebirla para que su poder absoluto también haya cambiado. Ella es la reina, y el cielo que cambia vertiginosamente para su mirada es el lugar más próximo al trono, al renacer. La herida hecha por el tiempo se enrojece y sana poco a poco con la luz. ¿Es mi madre, esa niña cuyos vellos púbicos perdieron su esplendor —esa piel blanca atravesada por ríos de várices; esa mujer que se avergüenza de estar cansada en un sillón—, y se aproxima cada vez más a la idea de su propia estatua? Su coquetería era de tanta naturalidad artificial, algo así como una fruta pintada, retocada —como el fondo del cielo de una cáscara contra el techo de cal. Algo insincero en el gesto de cubrirse la mitad de la pierna, el pelo, el disimulo, la sonrisa. (Coger el pliegue de la saya vitral con los dedos en pinza). Y en el doblez hay cariño, hay dolor... Un peine al final, rajado, percudido y plástico, como el frágil látigo de acariciar siempre hacia arriba, su única caricia entre el peine que sube y el dedo en tenaza que aprisiona el pliegue de una saya tensa siempre. Todo el mundo que ha vivido está allí, boca arriba, y lo mira de soslayo, sin atreverse a encararlo. ¡Dios, Dios! ¿Dónde se esconde la mujer bellísima y sin retocar del retrato limpio ahora por el programa digital? ¿Fue esta? ¿Fue siempre esta? ¿El envés de una reina? ¿Mi madre? ¿Su sillón de mimbre deshilachado, un trono? ¿La actriz que aún se prepara para su película en el doble de Annita Arwin? El

Jigs and Lures

The immense sky belonging to me collapsed on a detail of my prayer. I thought it was changing from yellows into intense fires. He lied. It was my perspective that had changed its angle. The rest will pass. Passion, life, the need to be held, the gift. All this useless pursuit of nothingness when a cloud is about to change its course, dissolve nothingness itself. He would stay there, stuck in his circumvallations, with his metaphors, with his light—maybe I'll see it someday. Cracks in the wall and heat lightning stand in for everything that's missing from this afternoon and she, my mother, like a sleepwalker, moves throughout the entire house too; it's round, circular, like a small tapestry. I think I'll already have a different formula for conceiving her, one that will change her absolute power. She is the queen, and the sky that changes dizzyingly under her gaze marks the location closest to the throne, to rebirth. The wound made by time reddens and heals little by little with the light. Is she my mother, that girl whose pubic hairs lost their splendor—white skin crossed by rivers of varicose veins; woman ashamed of being tired in an armchair—who gets closer and closer to the concept of her own stature? Her coquetry was of such an artificial naturalness, something like that, like a painted fruit, touched up—the orange rind sculpted on her ceiling, coated later in white paint. Something insincere in her gesture of half-covering her leg, her hair, her dissimulation, her smile. (Catching up the pleat of the turquoise skirt with fingers acting as pincers.) And in her folding, there is tenderness, there is pain... An old comb, cracked, plastic, dirtied, like the fragile domination expressed in gestures always moving upwards, her only caress located between the comb that pushes her hair back and the finger on the iron that imprisons the pleat of a perpetually taut skirt. The whole world that has ever lived is there, face up and looking sidelong at her, without daring to face her. God, God—where is the woman hidden, the beautiful one

tiempo no avanza, sino que retrocede, se curva. Ella estaba ahorita en la misma sala, sobre los mismos almohadones manchados. Pero en unos días, cientos de historias habrían pasado por su cuerpo atravesando la epidermis, llenándola de pequeñas manchas azuladas, agujeros casi a contraluz. *Cada pliegue de su cara es un retazo; cada contorno determina un sujeto (de plomo), un acontecimiento, para engañar.* Y allí estábamos todos los hijos malditos o preferidos; todos los pasados en los restos de un paisaje crepuscular cosido en su cojín de muaré. Encima, sus zapatos. *Más arriba, sus piernas delgadas, y después el cuerpo que alguien me quitaba entre las sábanas.* Creo que nunca la había visto así, tan de cerca, tan distante, dando una vuelta entera por la casa hasta llegar despacio y refugiarse en su sillón. *Sólo cuando entro al elevador oscuro —al túnel— y se la llevan hacia donde ya no puedo estar (a donde ya no soy nadie para permitirme, ni ella es mi madre) me sentía perdida, partida y aterrada.* Aterradoramente sola jugando con una jeringa vacía. *Cuando regresa, justo con el movimiento inverso hacia el sillón —que siempre le quito, que siempre le he quitado—, la bolsa de sangre aún cuelga de su brazo como un señuelo de plomo contra el tiempo, y me regaña:* "…qué estás haciendo aquí?"

who needs no digital retouching for a clean portrait? Was she this woman? Was she always this one? The flip side of a queen? My mother? Her fraying wicker armchair—a throne? The actress who continues to prepare for her movie, who looks like a double for Annita Arwin? Time does not advance; it recedes, it curves. Now she was in the same room, on the same stained pillows. But in a few days, hundreds of stories would have passed over her body, crossing the epidermis, filling it with small blue spots—almost holes, backlit. Each fold of her face is a remnant; each outline determines a subject (lead fishhook), an event, to create a deception. And there we were, all the damned or favorite children; all the pasts in the remains of a dusky landscape sewn into its moiré cushion. On top, her shoes. Above those, her thin legs, and then the body that someone took away from me wrapped in sheets. I don't think I had ever seen her this way, so close, so distant, making a circuit through the entire house until arriving slowly at her chair to find refuge. Only when I get into the dark elevator—the tunnel—and they take her to a place where I can't go (where I'm not someone who can be permitted, and she's not even my mother), I was feeling lost, split open, terrified. Terrifyingly alone, playing with an empty syringe. When she returns, making the exact inverse motion toward the chair—the one I always take from her, have always taken from her—the bag of blood still hangs from her arm like a leaden decoy to fool time, and she scolds me, "…what are you doing here?"

La tortuga del aula

para Elis

No es mentira que toco, toco, no la puerta,
ni la mesa con los nudillos flacos, ásperos,
si el pensamiento.
"Toco, pues pienso" —dijo ella—, las hendiduras
por donde circula un tono y otro de sangre,
el coágulo que vendrá (de cuarzo)
a matarme.
Pues mi hija me ha pedido una tortuga
que no cambie su carapacho,
o se fugue de sí
hacia el agua caliente y salitrosa
—por los cuadrados que de su dura piel antigua refractan
algo viscoso.
No es mentira que toco su carapacho blando
y otras cosas que no suenan por suerte:
(osadía de tocar por la voz, por la imaginación o el dolor)
y me separo rápido.
Como juntar los cuerpos no sé,
nunca he sabido,
paso la yema con gesto afectuoso
por dobleces, circunvalaciones.
Zding, zding, suena a metal sobre hierro,
pero ningún sonido que transfiera a este lugar
la sofoca.
La tortuguita fue transportada por una mano de niño
de la cubeta al suelo
y ha muerto al ser tocada.
Coágulo de cuarzo su coraza (la mente) abierta,
manoseada con irresponsabilidad se contrae

The classroom turtle

for Elis

This is no fiction—I'm tapping, tapping, not on the door,
not on the table with my narrow, rough knuckles
but on thought.
"I'm tapping, since I'm thinking," she said, of the cracks
where it circulates in one shade, in another shade,
the blood clot that will come (like a quartz)
to kill me.
So my daughter asked me for a turtle
that wouldn't trade out its shell
or escape
toward warm salinitrous water
—through the squares refracting some viscous thing
from its hard and ancient skin.
It's no fiction, that I tap on its soft carapace
and on other things that luckily make no sound:
(boldness of tapping with my voice, with my imagination or my
                                                              sorrow)
I pull away quickly.
Bringing bodies together is a skill I don't have,
never had.
With an affectionate gesture I run a fingertip
over deceits, roundabouts.
Zding, zding, it sounds like steel on iron,
but no sound that might transfer to this place
smothers it.
A child's hand transported the tiny turtle
from the pail to the ground,
and the turtle died after it was tapped.
Clot of quartz, its open cuirass (the mind)
contracts when handled roughly,

y su cara rosado beige asoma por debajo
de un llamado, lejos, lejos
—donde está también él—
con lo que fue su vida anterior bajo el carapacho
ahora azulado.
Por la abertura del techo baja un hilo de agua
sobre su vientre
decorado con amargura.
Olor a légamo en el aula.
Obsesión de separarse del chorro movedizo.
Así descubro su mancha
de la vulgar pertenencia.

and its rose-beige face peeps
out from under a cry, far away, far away
—where he too can be found—
the thing that used to be his former life
under a carapace, turned blue.
A thread of water descends from the hole in the ceiling
onto his belly
adorned in animus.
Odor of clay in the classroom.
Fixation with pulling away from the fickle crowd.
That's how I find his stain
from a communal kind of belonging.

Así tenía que ser

Soñó con un cachivache de madera clara,
de esas maderas viejas para pasar la mano y sentir
el hilo del árbol muerto que se desplaza
a fibra. Tocar el ser de la madera usada, sin barniz.
Ella y su hermano columpiándose con la arenilla abajo.
Lazos que se zafan de su espalda y otra mano que sostiene
una espiga. Quedar así, columpiándose en la foto gris,
arrimada a la madera más que antes
sin oír las conversaciones tan molestas, sin vecinos
—una edad en la que no se tiene con quien compartir las ganancias
porque ya sólo hay pérdidas.
El aire es tenso todavía porque teme caer desde esa altura,
y la espiga en la nariz pica un poco.
Volver sería incómodo.
Dejarla, con la mano sobre la madera
sentada en el columpio del portal,
loca por ver sus zapatos acharolados.
Dejarla, con la cabeza caída sobre el hombro, inclinada.
No la despierten.
No vengan a buscarla.
Déjenla disfrutar que nadie pueda venir
a estas altas horas del tiempo y de los años.
La espiga silenciosa cae y se pierde también con la arenilla.
Borrasca es todo cuanto tiene, borrasca,
se mece
y, luego,
cae.

How it had to be

She dreamed about a trinket made of pale wood,
one of those aged woods over which you run your hand, feeling
threads from the dead tree pass through
the fibers. Fingering the presence of wood used like this,
                                                    untreated.
She and her brother swinging above, powdery sand below.
Loops that slip from her back and another hand holding
a dry spike of grass. To stay like that, swinging inside the gray
                                                    photo,
joined to the wood more than ever before
without hearing the irritable conversations, without neighbors
—a time when you have no one to split the earnings
because there are only losses.
The air still feels tense because she fears falling from that height,
and the spike poking her nose smarts a little.
Going back would be uncomfortable.
Leaving her with a hand on the wood,
sitting on the swing by the door,
wild about her polished shoes.
Leaving her with her head tilted, fallen on her shoulder.
Don't wake her.
Don't come looking for her.
Let her enjoy the fact that no one could come
so late at night and after so many years.
The spike falls; it too disappears silently in the sand.
Upheaval is all she has left, upheaval,
she rocks
then
falls.

Sentada en el Parque de los Enamorados

Estuvo sentada junto a los caballos.
El pequeño caballo de la melena blanca, la miraba.
De pronto, un olor a yerba quemada con carbón,
un ligero hollín proveniente del sur
tocó su espalda. No era la dueña del negocio,
pero alguien al pasar le preguntó por otros potros.
Mientras acariciaba al pequeño animal
sintió aquel olor penetrar sus pulmones
y al belfo acariciar levemente su costado.
Era un caballo muy joven.
Soltó todas sus amarras,
pero el potro continuó a su lado, fiel.

(En casa de Chichí se cocinaba con un gran anafe en el patio.)
Recordó los pedazos de carbón encendidos
durante las tardes de verano.
No tenía imágenes para sustituir
un olor perdido a yerba que se quema.
Tocó levemente los ojos del animal
que tenía una herida en la mejilla
y sangraba. Como ella, recostado contra una reja,
se había herido al pasar.
Sintió escalofríos y pensó en su infancia.
El tiempo que le había costado llegar hasta aquí.
A la traición de olvidarse y ser olvidada,
opuso aquella resistencia de la fidelidad
de un animal extraño que te acaricia y se queda sin nada.
El potro pegó saliva gruesa sobre sus manos.
Ningún ser humano la había acariciado así, jamás.

Sitting in Sweethearts Park

She was sitting by the horses.
The tiny horse with the white mane was watching her.
A sudden odor of burnt grass and charcoal;
a light southern ash
grazed her back. She didn't own the paddock
but a passerby asked her about other colts.
As she stroked the little animal
she felt that smell penetrate her lungs,
and his lip touched her side, gently.
He was a very young horse.
She let go of all his reins,
but the colt stayed at her side, loyal.

(At Nana's house they cooked with a big grill on the patio.)
She remembered pieces of glowing charcoal
on summer evenings.
She had no images to substitute
for the lost odor of burning grass.
She touched the animal's eyes, gently;
there was a wound on his cheek
and it bled. Like her, leaning against a railing,
he had hurt himself along the way.
She shivered and thought about her childhood.
The time it had cost to get this far.
She resisted the betrayal of forgetting herself, being forgotten,
with the fidelity of an unknown animal
who rubs against you and gets nothing in return.
The colt left thick saliva on her hands.
No human had ever caressed her like that. Ever.

La madre, el piano

Dejo el libro de Marina sobre el piano.
Con el último acorde, muere su ilusión
en mi mano.
Muerta de su texto resurge sobre el mío (ebria)
"...aluhete, siempre aluhete..."
La razón estalla entre la vena abultada
de la mano y el vaso.
Tómala, joven de pelo rizo y profundas ojeras.
Es la mano equivocada.
No tengo tiempo para ti,
no traigo nada.
La vena estalla y la sangre a borbotones
baja por el hilo del brazo. Su música
clavetea mi espalda y la amordaza.
No me puedo entregar así.
Nunca más.

Delirio en el beso robado, entre las comisuras,
en el vientre.
"¡Si puedo ser tu madre!"
Me viro en la butaca y toco
aquellas notas sueltas en el giro
de una agria melodía endulzada.
"Soy tu madre, Marina, soy tu madre,
y me he llevado tu música a la sangre."
Tiene un color de cera en las mandíbulas,
aprieta el pedal, abre la octava.
El beso desprendido cae de su boca, ladeado.
(El beso está en mi infancia con sabor café
—no de azafrán o sándalo—,
pero la manera de estremecernos obra en la mente, igual.)

The mother, the piano

I leave Marina's book on the piano.
With the final chord, her final
illusion dies in my hand.
Dead, she reemerges from her text over mine (drunk)
"...alouette, always alouette..."
Reason explodes between the bulging vein
of her hand and my drinking glass.
Take it, young man, with your curly hair, deep circles under
                                        your eyes.
It's the wrong hand.
I don't have time for you,
didn't bring anything.
The vein explodes and the blood comes
spewing down my arm. Her mother's music
adorns my back and silences her.
I can't give in like that.
Never again.

Delirium in the stolen kiss, between the corners of the mouth,
in the abdomen.
"If I can be your mother!"
I turn in the armchair and play
those single notes in the transfer
of a bitter melody made sweet.
"I'm your mother, Marina, I'm your mother,
and I've carried your music in my blood."
A waxy color to her jaws, she
steps on the pedal, opens the octave.
The generous kiss falls from her mouth, tilted.
(In my childhood the kiss tastes like coffee
—not saffron or sandalwood—
but our way of shuddering with the work in our minds is the same.)

"Tú con la espina dorsal, yo con la vena cortada
puedo morir de poner al diablo sobre el piano."
Ojos dorados, albaricoque … ¡que mienten!
¿Cómo relaciono este beso con la despedida de mi padre
y de la infancia?

La niña nunca dejó
ese pasillo interminable
del teclado
(por eso ni poeta ni pianista fui).
Perseguida que en su persecución
se vuelve eterna novia de tu amante.
"Hombre de pelo rizo, tienes potestad para zafar
los lazos, las costumbres…
Toma el vino y escapa."
Hay sangre coagulada bajo su comisura.
Horror de sellar (besando) un pacto con el diablo,
mientras la música acromática
con sus cien años de perversión la alcanza.
"Afinidad por la infinitud de una sintonía" —dices,
y no comprendo nada.

Otro acorde para que se suspenda
la estabilidad de la muerte.
Prórroga fatal de un silencio a otro.
"Valían quince pesos sin comisión, lo sabes."
Demasiado dinero para el equilibrio de una vida.
Pon de nuevo tu boca de martinete
y resucita.
"Marina, mi niña —advierte a mi oído
contra el soplo del viento sur, la madre—.
Son días de invierno verdadero o falso.
Te he dicho que el hombre de cejas anchas
viene a buscarte."

"You with the spine, me with the open vein
I can die from putting the devil on the piano."
Golden eyes, apricot… they lie!
How do I connect this kiss to goodbyes for my father
and my childhood?

The girl never left
that interminable hallway,
the keyboard
(the reason I was neither poet nor pianist).
Hunted, within her hunted state she becomes
the woman eternally betrothed to your lover.
"Curly-haired man, you have the authority to loose
ropes, customs…
Drink your wine and make your escape."
There's coagulated blood under the corner of his mouth.
Horror of sealing a pact with the devil (through a kiss),
while the colorless music
reaches her with its one hundred years of perversion.
"Affinity for the infinitude of a tuning knob," you say,
and I don't understand at all.

Another chord, so the stability of death
will be suspended.
Fatal deferment from one silence to another.
"They were worth fifteen pesos uncommissioned, you know."
Too much money for the balance of a life.
Put on your martinet mouth
and come back to life.
"Marina, my daughter," the mother warns
at my ear, against the breath of southern wind.
"These are days of winter, whether real or false.
I told you: the wide-browed man
is coming for you."

Su música

La partitura estará vacía.
En ella no aparecerá nada.
Como Constance comerá castañas romanas
y tú serás el genio.
Desapasionado, no persuasivo.
Una línea en blanco y sobre ella, de repente:
fagot, clarinete,
en el corazón de las muchachas que sonríen.
Hacia un espacio ascendente
(mordido por su boca)
el licor de la castaña ahora vacía, quieta.
Hay demasiadas notas esperándonos.
Opacos rumbos que tomaron los sonidos
de un destino.

Her music

The score will be empty.
Nothing will appear on it.
Like Constance, she'll eat Roman chestnuts
and you'll be the genius.
Impartial, not persuasive.
A blank line and on it, suddenly:
bassoon, clarinet
in the hearts of smiling girls.
Rising toward a space
(bitten out by her mouth)
liquor from the chestnut, now emptied, quiet.
Too many notes wait for us.
Gloomy paths that took the sound
out of a destination.

Si hubiera tenido…

para Ana

Si hubiera tenido una nana
que se llamara Ana
y supiera mecerme
en sus rodillas,
la melancolía de su canción preferida
me acompañaría hasta el final.
(Una infancia de canción sin fin.)

Tú hubieras debido llegar antes.
Salir del vil tiempo
de las cosas imposibles.
Pero son tan jóvenes,
¡tan endemoniadamente jóvenes!
Todo debió ser de otra manera.
Pero sin nana y sin ti,
¿cómo escondo la tarde cayendo contra mi ventana?
¿La abro totalmente?
¿La escondo detrás del librero
sin dejarla salir?

De los deseos, nada sé.
Sólo acumularlos en el estuche de un después mecánico
(ecos de una respiración que jadea en silencio).
¿Por qué no vienes y me engañas?
¿Por qué no traes una nana
que me acune otra vez
al despertar?
¿Otra trama tendida en el recuerdo?
No me verá crecer
ni me arropará en las noches

If I'd had...

for Ana

If I'd had a nanny
named Annie
and learned how to rock
upon her knees,
her favorite song's melancholy
would stay with me to the end.
(A never-ending childhood of song.)

You would have had to arrive earlier.
Exiting the vile tempo
of impossibilities.
But they're so young,
so devilishly young!
Everything was going to happen a different way.
But without a nanny and without you,
how do I hide the evening falling against my window?
Do I open it all the way?
Do I hide it behind the bookshelf
and stop it from getting out?

About desires I know nothing.
Just accumulating them in the box of a mechanical afterwards
(echoes of breathing that heaves in silence).
Why don't you show up and deceive me?
Why don't you bring a nanny
to cradle me again
when I wake?
Another fraud stretching through memory?
She won't see me grow
or tuck me in during my nights

51

de desvelo y de frío.
Y sin ella, la posibilidad de tu llegada será también
incierta.
Porque no tengo "formas de llamar desde el olvido…"
Volverá el dolor y tendré insomnio.

¿Quieres venir a cantarme,
a engañarme otra vez?
Tal vez voy a morir,
y las mujeres cuando van a morir
quieren oír su última canción.
"Arrópame…,
me pierdo dentro de un cuerpo ajeno
y envilezco.
Un vals, ¿no lo oyes…?, tocan un vals."
Mientras la nana se va, tan vieja de mi lado,
indiferente a una infancia sin canción
ni fin.

of insomnia and cold.
And without her, the possibility of your arrival will also be
uncertain.
Because I don't have "ways of calling out from oblivion..."
The pain will return and I'll be sleepless.

Do you want to come and sing to me,
deceive me one more time?
Maybe I'm going to die,
and when women are going to die
they want to hear their final song.
"Tuck me in...,
I lose myself inside a foreign body
and am debased.
A waltz, don't you hear it...? they're playing a waltz."
While the nanny moves away, so old, from my side,
indifferent to a childhood without a song
or an ending.

Suena el silbato

El hombre viejo sobre la pista de cemento
recoge la pelota. Un solo gesto
y está caliente el brazo del lanzamiento.
La pelota rebota y cae
bajo el banco donde he pretendido establecer mi dominio
de observador.
La estoy mirando caer hacia la fuga del presente conmigo.
Un joven atleta desfigura el hombro, la pierna, su caída.
Ha vuelto a poner su cuerpo ante la malla de mi visión
y el olvido.
(Era poca cosa lo que teníamos
si no lo aprovechábamos bien.)

El aire denso desvía la pelota que golpea
mi cabeza atolondrada.
Sobre la pista de cemento
tuercas pequeñas, desfloraciones,
escarabajos por la periferia de mi obsesión.
Un aire frío roza la comisura izquierda de mi boca
que aún intenta sonreír.
Qué habrá pasado en este día,
en esto justo e injusto momento de perder?
La pelota golpea sin fuerza
y cae.
Pura avería del deseo,
de la monotonía del existir.

El hombre de la pelota gris y el joven atleta
se han ido
(cada uno tras su tiempo),
fantasmas de una tarde de abril.
Y yo, me habré quedado allí?

The whistle blows

The old man picks up a baseball in a concrete lot
used for street games. A single move
and his throwing arm is warm.
The ball bounces and drops
under the bench where I've been trying to establish my
dominion
as observer.
I'm watching it drop with me, toward some escape from the
present.
A young athlete twists his shoulder, his leg, its fall.
He wedges his body in front of my vision, its mesh,
and oblivion.
(We had almost nothing
unless we made really good use of it.)

The thick air deflects the ball and it hits
my muddled head.
Nuts and bolts, deflowerings
all over the concrete track,
beetles around the periphery of my obsession.
A cold breeze scrapes against the left corner of my mouth
which is still trying to smile.
What has happened on this day,
in this just and unjust instant of loss?
The ball thuds weakly
and drops.
Pure collapse of desire,
monotony of existence.

The man with the ball, gray, and the young athlete
went away
(each one after his moment),
phantoms of an April evening.
And me: Will I have stayed there?

Catch and release

...el anzuelo de la voluntad de las limaduras del ser...

Artaud

PARA FRANK LEÓN

Coger y dejar sin que el anzuelo penetre,
detener un momento al pez entre los dedos,
acariciar es demasiado gesto,
y poseer, un crimen.
Yo diría tocar de un modo diferente
que podría ser áspero al contacto de la primera vez
sin apartar la espina que provoca la escama.
(La espina es la mentira.)
Tiempo de lo perdido andaba buscando
un límite del tacto.
He visto peces que naufragan como hombres,
conchas deshechas
y la mala palabra del animal
que agota su intención entre los dedos.
He dicho escama
para no decir ausencia del deseo
de tocar aquellas cosas
trascendentes.

Catch and release

...hook for the will, made from the filings of the self...

Artaud

FOR FRANK LEÓN

To catch and release so the hook doesn't penetrate,
to hold the fish between your fingers for the moment,
caressing is too grand a gesture,
possession, a crime.
I would call it a different way of touching
which can be harsh at first
but doesn't remove the spine that agitates the scale.
(The spine is the lie.)
In a time of something now lost, I tried to find
the limit to the sense of touch.
I have seen fish who sink like men,
conchs shattered
and the curse of the animal
who exhausts its sense of purpose between my fingers.
I've said scale
so as not to say absence of the desire
to touch things that are
transcendent.

Pescadores, crudos

para J. A. Miralles

No es láudano lo que van a sacar
del fondo ocre de tu espera
en el muro.
Bajo, muy abajo, al fondo,
se descompone y fracciona el pensamiento.
Cadáveres de peces, sombras y luces
que antes fueron perfiles de barcos
—hierros fundidos de la imaginación
que la costa salvaje ha reducido
a esa miseria de contaminación
sin ser ya nada,
chatarra para depredadores.

Busco el movimiento del hilo de nylon
porque quiero recuperar la historia hundida y así,
los veo halar algo que fue inconstante
desde el potro del muro con su pesar a flote.
Pero a flote no viene otra vez la vida en su barco,
y no se ha pescado suficiente para atravesar esta calma chicha
que engaña con su lapso a la tempestad.
Cuando la tarde se va de tu visión de hacerla
contra el rostro de esos pescadores
de camisas casi pardas,
recordándonos
que algo salvaje y especial
con pellejo lustroso al sol
no pescarán.

Fishermen, rough

for J. A. Miralles

It's not laudanum they'll pull out
of the ochreous depths of your patience
waiting on the wall.
Deeper, much deeper, at the bottom,
thought decomposes and breaks apart.
Fish corpses, shadows of lights
that once marked ships' profiles
—shackles forged from the imagination
reduced by the wild coast
to the wretchedness of pollution
not being anything anymore,
scrap iron for scavengers.

I watch for movement on the nylon line
because I want to recover sunken history, and so
I see them haul out something changeable,
the fishermen riding the wall like horsemen, their heavy grief
afloat.
But life doesn't come floating past a second time in its boat
and there hasn't been enough fishing to navigate this dead calm
that deceives us by lapsing into storms.
When the afternoon vacates the vision you were creating of it
over the faces of those fishermen
in their work-browned shirts,
reminding us
they can't fish out
a wild and special something
with a skin that would shine in the sun.

Giotakus

En el vientre de la ballena, en el mío,
una sensación de inmensidad vacía.
No traigo peces muertos, no he comido las frutas del fondo
preferidas.
No he digerido más que el árido color de los corales.
Comida cortante, polvo de hueso, cartílago que hiere.
Me paseo sin profundidad, y con vértigo
respiro agitada o pausada, siempre artificial
esperando una mano blanca que acaricie mi lomo plateado.
Si una ola volviera a mecerme contra los arrecifes!, luego
vendré a morir. Seré despellejada y repartida
como carne cualquiera entre la gente.
Recuerdo cómo salía para vigilar el horizonte y despertaba
con el canto de algas. Algo creí ver a relieve y moviéndose
entre aquella inmensidad que era mi casa al fondo del océano.
Ahora, arrastrada por el conocimiento de mi cuerpo espeso,
enredada en un fondo miserable,
a quién iré a pertenecer?
No quiero alimentar al extraño consuelo
del arponazo final de la alimaña.
Prefiero fingir que me he quedado ausente de la profundidad.
Alelada y constante entre pequeños peces.

Gyotaku

In the belly of the whale, in mine,
a sensation of hollow immensity.
No dead fish there. I haven't eaten the best foods from
the ocean floor.
The dry colorations of coral are all I've digested.
Bitter fruit, meal of bone, cartilage trailing wounds.
I move without depth, in vertigo
I breathe, agitated or deliberate, always artificial
waiting for a pale hand to run down my silver spine.
If a wave would rock me back against the reef! So
will I come to death. I will be flayed and divided
as any other flesh among the people.
I remember watching over the horizon and waking
to the chant of algae. Something I thought I saw in relief and
                                            moving
through that immensity, my home on the seafloor.
Now dragged by knowledge of my thick body,
tangled in a miserable profundity,
at whose disposal will I be?
I don't want to nurture the strange consolation
of a final harpooning by a scavenger.
I'd rather pretend to have remained absent from the profound
                                                  depths.
Astonished and constant among the lesser fish.

¡Vaya, Colibrí!

Para Edgar

Vaya, Colibrí, no te hagas el loco.
¡Arrea!, carga tu carretón.
Soy la mujer que bajó de la colina esta mañana.
Estoy sentada en tu carretón y voy hacia la zona.
La zona se aproxima al carretón.
El sonido de la zona me estremece.
¿Cómo describir el traqueteo del caballo
aproximándome a ti
—ancha franja de cemento
y un girasol marchito dentro de un pomo oval?
"Cualquier lugar tiene su amuleto allí,
donde menos lo esperamos" —respondes.

No logro el sonido que me lleva
de la zona a la mistificación.
(…tathata… tathata…)
Hay alambres de púa con alta tensión.
Ayer estaba muy lejos
jugando a ser la escritora o la actriz.
Hoy soy otro personaje en esta región
(de la desesperación),
Colibrí, un personaje real.
No te hagas el loco.
¡Arrea! herido por el girasol que dejó de ser un mito.
Desbocado por la mala fe.
Derrotado por la herida del sol en la pata.
El prisionero revienta su boca cruda de caballo.
Tiene el pelo amarillo de la tarde
y besa sus pétalos como si fueran sombras de árboles.
Estoy rodeada de estiércol.

Really, Hummingbird!

for Edgar

Really, Hummingbird, don't be a fool.
Come on! Load your cart.
I'm the woman who came down the hill this morning.
I'm sitting on your cart, riding toward that zone.
That zone is closing in on the cart.
The sound from the zone makes me shudder.
How can I describe the way the horse clip-clops
as I come closer to you
—wide cement strip,
wilted sunflower in an oval bottle?
"Every place contains its amulet,
where we least expect it," you respond.

I can't capture the sound that carries me
from that zone toward mystification.
(…tathata… tathata…)
Barbed wires, high voltage.
Yesterday I was very far away,
playing writer or actress.
I am a different character in this region (of desperation) today:
Hummingbird, I'm a real person.
Don't be a fool.
Come on! You were wounded by a sunflower that's no longer
mythological.
Struck dumb by bad faith.
Struck down by the wound from the sun on your foot.
The prisoner's rude horse-mouth splits open.
He holds the afternoon's downy yellow
and kisses its petals as though they were shadows cast by trees.
Manure surrounds me.

"No llores, Colibrí, espera por mí" —*le cantas*
ante la oprobiosa necesidad
¿trascendente?

"Don't cry, Hummingbird, wait for me," you sing to her,
faced with need: inglorious.
transcendent?

Invenio

No puedo ser caballo
aunque busque refugio en las caballerizas,
aunque finja un relincho.
No puedo ser sol aunque queme y alumbre
la extensión de una vida.
Lo natural ha muerto
(porque no puedo inventar su devenir)
como justifico la arbitrariedad de cada palabra
en su desvarío.
Qué puedo ser entonces (o parecer que soy)
si tampoco puedo ser bosque y sacudirme contra el viento
o helarme?

El bosque se aproximó tanto que se volvió escombro de pinos
y robles cortados.
Lo que ves es un cuadro de la desfloración.
Lo que ves es la llama ceniza del sol,
el ojo prohibido del caballo muerto por la tentación.
Lo que ves ya no existe.

Winterbane

I can't be a horse
even if I seek shelter in stables,
even if I fake a neigh.
I can't be a sun even if I set fires and light up
the expanse of a lifetime.
The natural part has died
(because I can't invent its transfiguration)
as I justify the arbitrary state of every word
in its incoherence.
So what can I be (or seem to be)
if I can't be a forest to rattle against the wind,
to ice over?

The forest came so close that it turned to pine debris
with cut oaks.
What you see is a portrait of a deflowering.
What you see is the sun's ashen flame,
the forbidden eye of a horse slaughtered by temptation.
What you see no longer exists.

Canto del huérfano

Si un hombre da pan y cerezo a los mirlos,
si no sale de su cuerpo para verlos crecer
y se encierra en su obstinada paz
cuando empieza el verano
—un hombre encerrado en la tela-yerba del vacío—
dónde puedo encontrar su corazón?,
dónde estalla su fiebre entre la madrugada
y el miedo probatorio de la sinrazón?
No queda nada más que esa imagen borrosa
de sol que declina en el surco del labio.
Un labio que besa a cualquier distancia de la realidad.

Salido de un texto escrito por él mismo esta mañana,
aburrido de comprender cosas
(de trastear el espectáculo),
desolado, se encorva un poco más,
reclina su pensamiento absoluto y ya no finge
que quiere jugar contra el abandono.
Se abandona, porque él también ha sido conquistado.
"Haced conmigo lo que queráis" —ha dicho.

El desplazado de cualquier conquista
es seducido por la tentación más cara: la renuncia.
Ha renunciado a ser, a poseer, a creer.
Cambia de hotel, de paisaje, de equipaje.
Está en un sin lugar.
(Nada supera al espectáculo de su vacío.)
Y, en el vacío como realidad,
espera simplemente
a que crezcan los mirlos.

Orphan's song

If a man gives bread and a cherry tree to the blackbirds
if he doesn't leave his body to see them grow,
if he encloses himself in his obstinate peace
as summer begins
—a man confined in a plaited-grass void—
where can I find his heart?
where does his fever explode, between dawn
and a probative fear of outrage?
Nothing is left but a blurry image
of the sun setting on his furrowed lip.
A lip brushing past at some distance from reality.

Projected out of a text he himself wrote this morning
bored by comprehending things
(by messing around with spectacle),
gutted, he stoops a little more,
allows his absolute thinking to relax, and no longer pretends
he wants to defy resignation.
He resigns himself, because he too has been conquered.
"Do with me as you will," he said.

Displaced by conquest one
is seduced by the most costly of temptations: renunciation.
He renounces existence, possession, belief.
He changes hotels, landscapes, luggage.
He occupies a non-place.
(Nothing beats the spectacle of his own void.)
And inside that void as reality,
he's just waiting
for blackbirds to grow.

El terral

Cada viento entra por una ventana diferente
según la edad.
Este, de los muertos,
se va llevando a la familia.
Atraviesa la flor que pongo más alta,
"flor de mi hermano" —la llamo—
en un búcaro de porcelana blanco.
Después, pasan los otros,
los que arrasan sentimientos
y te llevan, una a una, las palabras,
cuando pasan desde el fondo
decididos a no dejarte nada.
Y quieres recordar el nombre de una persona amada
o el sitio del encuentro (un olor)
cuando rastreas
nada!

El terral me enferma.
A veces, sabe quedarse líquido
tras la cortina transparente
y acaricia.
Después regresa inquieto,
florea en la madrugada,
trastea otros rincones
(hace un ruidito perspicaz),
al fin, encuentra dónde te escondes
y aniquila.
Es un viento dentro de la cabeza
que clavetea y clavetea
sin una pulgada de sosiego al despertar.

Breeze over the land

Each wind enters through a different window
according to the age.
This one belonging to the dead
keeps taking family away.
It slips through the flower I set highest up,
"my brother's flower"—I call it—
in a white porcelain boccaro pot.
Later other winds pass through.
sweep feelings away,
and carry your words, one by one,
as they move out of the backdrop
determined to leave you nothing.
And if you want to remember the name of someone you love
or the location of encounter (a scent)
and you follow its tracks—
nothing!

The breeze makes me ill.
Sometimes it can turn liquid
through the transparent curtain
and nuzzle up.
Later it returns, restless,
blossoms at dawn,
roams through other corners
(makes a shrewd little sound),
finds you wherever you're hiding in the end
and annihilates.
It's a wind inside the head
driving in studs as decoration,
leaving not an inch of serenity when you wake.

Junto a ella

Completando una frase perdida
en su rompecabezas de cartón va
(ensanchándose)
hacia la inexistencia.
También tenía una imagen mental
—menor, antigua, trémula, insignificante—
y su constante representación.
Ahora latía su aorta con vehemencia.
Era su actriz predilecta.

Su cara absoluta le devolvió una imagen errada.
Esa señora frente a él
que lo miraba insistentemente, ¿era ella?
Oblicua, ¿quién sería?
¿En qué año nació?
¿Cuándo se puso así?
¿Después de la confesión?
Ya no se reconocía.
Ortodoxa, no se permitía arrastrar
una postura colegial por tanto tiempo
sobre el río de lava volcánica
de aquella presencia.

En el banco, mientras ella le explicaba
letras del follaje, arrepentimientos,
estaba fría, pero si él acercaba su rodilla
(como una manta)
estaría tibia en un momento.
¿Cuánto dura un roce en la mente?
¿Cuánto tiempo esperó para esto?
¡Qué sarcasmo!

At her side

Finishing an idle phrase
in her jigsaw puzzle she moves
(stretching)
toward nonexistence.
She too used to have a mental image
—lesser, ancient, flickering, insignificant—
and her unvarying representation.
Now her aorta thumped furiously.
That actress used to be her favorite.

Her face, absolute, rejected a false image.
This lady in front of him
who would stare at him so insistently: Was it her?
Oblique, who was she?
In what year was she born?
When did she get that way?
After confessing?
No longer recognizable.
Orthodox, she didn't allow herself to grovel
in schoolgirl positions for so long
over the river of lava
from that remote presence.

On the bench, as she explained to him
letters in the verbiage, regrets,
she was cold, but if he drew one knee closer
(like a blanket)
she flushed with warmth.
How long does a light touch last in the mind?
How long did she wait for this?
So sarcastic!

Se le había arrugado, de repente, el entrecejo.
"¿Por qué no existiría la verdadera detención del tiempo?" —repetía.

Estaba (ridícula) y vencida,
con su sombrerito sonrisa paja hambrienta
que se había malogrado por el desinterés
en el banco de mármol caliente (ya, la tumba)
esperando una satisfacción tardía,
otra aceptación.
Él se reía, y se reía...
porque sabía lo que ella estaba sintiendo,
pero fingía que no tenía miedo
y la dejaba con el pecado
de la perversión del tiempo
—la única perversión inevitable—
junto a ella.

One brow suddenly wrinkled.
"Why couldn't time truly be arrested?"—she would repeat.

She was ridiculous and defeated,
with her little hat smile puff of hungry delusion
that had miscarried through indifference
on the warm marble bench (already the tomb)
waiting for a deferred satisfaction,
another acceptance.
He laughed and laughed...
because he knew what she was feeling
but pretended he wasn't scared
and left her with the sin
of time's perversion
—the singular, inevitable perversion—
by her side.

Rear Window

Va alejándose, alejándose,
desapareciendo hacia el final de un texto, ella,
"…la dueña de un rechazo…" —*como él la nombró.*
Ella, con uvas frescas en la mano izquierda (aún sin tocar)
sabe que es de pronto olvidada,
sacada de la ficción de una ventana indiscreta
y sustituida.
Pero no es ella quien se aleja
hacia la esquina del paisaje.
No puede oponer su cuerpo allí,
donde estuvo la otra años atrás,
recogiendo "maneras de sentir",
adverbios (poses) en su banco de cemento
frente al túnel.
Nadie la vio apretar sus manos en el corto intento
de morir.
Ella, "…con los ojos de la amada…"
(desapareciendo del texto)
insignificante y podada por la sombra.
Foto de chica rubia
que hoy vive junto a él.
La casa sin paredes
y esa actriz muda, adentro
(como cualquier inquilina)
tomada de la mano para habitar la taquilla
y morir desangrada sobre la tela
al término de la esfera de una vida.
Hago un paneo hacia el parque
(frontal)
y ella se ha quedado sola
junto al hierro pulido que va de la baranda
al vidrio

Rear Window

Drifting away, drifting away,
fading at the tail end of a text, she,
"...mistress of a particular rejection...," as he titled her.
She, fresh grapes in her left hand (untouched),
knows she is abruptly forgotten,
deleted from the fiction of an indiscreet exit
and replaced.
But she's not the one drifting away
toward the corner of the landscape.
She can't counter the body there,
where the other woman once was, years ago,
collecting "ways of feeling,"
adverbs (poses) on her cement bench
facing the tunnel.
No one saw her clench her fists in a brief attempt
to die.
She, "...with eyes of the beloved..."
(fading from the text)
insignificant, clipped out by the shade.
Photo of the blonde
who lives with him now.
The house without walls
and that silent actress inside
(like any other uninvited guest)
taken by the hand to inhabit the pigeonhole
and die bleeding on a canvas
at the completion of one life's circuit.
I pan toward the park
(frontal angle)
and she ended up alone
by the polished iron that runs from rail
to store window

(renunciando a su imagen para transformarse
en hecho).
Porque ningún amigo trajo nunca
comida para gatos, ratoncitos,
peces muertos a través de la nieve, último intento
por sobrevivir.
Por lo que empezó a sospechar de alguien
que ni siquiera la vio
con su pequeño recipiente, esperando.

La imagen de su soledad sí se ha transformado
en un hecho rotundo,
carcomiendo esa ventana
—como en la película de Hitchcock (1954)—
donde la vimos aparecer (empinarse)
como una divinidad convertida en otra.
Junto a su oído, tu boca
rozando la distancia,
y ese árbol mezquino, la penumbra,
del breve amor a una reina.

(renouncing her image in order to transform
into fact).
Because no friend ever appeared through the snow
bringing food for the cats—little mice,
dead fish—any final attempt
at survival.
Whereupon she began to suspect someone
who didn't even see her
with her little container, waiting.

The image of her solitude did transform
into a resounding fact,
eating away at the window
—as in Hitchcock's film (1954)—
where we saw her appear (on tiptoe)
like one divinity converted into another.
Next to her ear, your mouth
brushing up against the distance,
and that miserable little tree, the semidarkness
from your short-lived, sovereign love.

Esculturas

Y, en el jardín, entre las esculturas,
hombres vaciados.
Restos de un yeso seco
entre los dientes.
A sus espaldas
(indiferente al deseo)
la pose indigna de envejecer.
Talla otro molde
con frágil pose,
hasta saciarse de perder
el sólido tiempo que la vence.
"...Agárrenme si pueden —les grita—,
no me van a coger..."

Sculptures

And, in the garden, among the sculptures,
castings: men.
Remains of dried plaster
between their teeth.
Their backs
humiliated by the angles of aging
(indifferent to desire).
She carves another mold
into a fragile pose
until she becomes satiated by the loss
of a solid form for the time conquering her.
"...Catch me if you can," she shouts at them,
"you're not going to get me..."

Mármoles

Él pregunta sobre mármoles.
"Te los llevaste todos al fin del mundo, a tu casa?"
Ni una vasija ajena, nada?
No recogiste aquello, rostros, algo?
La fuente vacía
y los bloques que bajaban
desde la roca al patíbulo
sin sentir su posesión.
Dice que fue en Carrara
(martillando seis años)
contra la tierra que no daba otra suposición, un golpe.
Nada trajiste con los años,
salvo el horror de olvidar.
Y él no puede comprender
que tus brazos no recogieran polvo,
desperdicio de antiguos brillos,
ni hombres que subían para morir contigo.

Pero tu boca decía...
"necesidad de hallar, necesidad de querer..."
Lo supe al comenzar la bajada.
Que haría este viaje (y aquel)
dentro de unos ojos rozando
órbitas que vieron precipitar los bloques,
en caída libre contra el viento.
Allí, los árboles, las heladas,
los amarillos peces confusos de la razón
quebrarse contra el río,
sin llevarse otra cosa
que arena o sal
del brusco golpe al pulir

Pieces in marble

He asks about pieces in marble.
"Did you bring them all to the end of the world, to your house?"
Not one pot from a foreign land, nothing?
You didn't get that thing, or faces, or anything?
The empty fountain
and the blocks they carried down
from the rock to the gallows
with no sense of possession.
He says it was in Carrara
(six years of hammering)
against earth that offered no other premise, a blow.
You collected nothing with the years
except a horror of oblivion.
And he can't understand
that your arms didn't gather dust,
residue from ancient polishings,
or men ascending in order to die with you.

But your mouth was reciting…
"need to find, need to want…"
I figured it out when I started my descent.
What this journey (and that other one) would do
within eyes grazing
orbits, eyes that saw the blocks plunge
into freefall against the wind.
There, the trees, the frosts,
the hazy yellow fish of the ratio
cracking against a river,
taking no more
than sand or salt
from the sharp blow refining

un crepúsculo y luego otro,
de pura gravedad,
de horror después!

one twilight, then another,
the pure gravity,
then horror!

Desde arriba, abajo

Rabieta, porque no tengo mesa transversal
laqueada
y la pasión arqueándose.
La maleta (no la giba) de sentir lo que se siente
—que a veces no es lo que nos proponemos querer sentir.
Luego, el cuerpo moldeado, abriéndose,
sobre una alfombra con espinas pequeñas
hincando al costado, el vientre.
Daba gusto alternar (esa oscuridad)
sin ser devueltos
jamás del suelo, envuelta en seda.
"No volveré, no volveré de allí."
Regazo es una palabra sin naturaleza, amanerada, frágil,
que no tiene la negrura filosa de aquella laca
pegándose fría (y sudada) a la espalda.
El ovillo que se cierra sobre la cintura (un torno)
de fatalidad para cortar.
He sido regazo, no corte mineral.

Decir que siento, he mentido.
Ni laca negra o protuberancias.
Nada de flejes que ablanden la tensión fingida
de resistir. Abajo, nada.
Sólo un cuerpo sobre la mesa (desmenuzado)
—en China, sobre ese Océano vertical—
amarra mi estupidez contra otra imagen
de ojos rasgados (cínicos)
que supieron mentir
y regodearse.
Mentí, no tuve mesa ni cumbre laqueada.
Y ya no hay tiempo para arquear el músculo
sobre un óvalo muerto.

Vertical cut

Rage, because I don't have
a lacquered crosscut table
or a passion, body arching.
The baggage (not the nuisance) is feeling what you feel
—which sometimes isn't what we tell ourselves we want to feel.
Then the molded body, opening
on a carpet with tiny spines
pricking your side, your belly.
It felt good to alternate (that darkness)
without ever being
brought back from the floor, wrapped in silk.
"I won't return, won't return from there."
Regazo is an unnatural word for the lap, formal and fragile,
without the sharp blackness of the lacquer
sticking, cold (and sweaty), to your back.
The curled body encircles the waist (a wheel)
of fate to make its cut.
I've been this maternal lap, not an angular stone.

Saying that I feel, I've lied.
No black lacquer or bulges.
No springs that might soften the false tension
of resistance. Underneath, nothing.
Only a body spread across the table (picked apart)
—in China, over that vertical Ocean—
binds my idiocy to another image
of almond-shaped eyes (cynical ones)
that figured out how to deliver lies
and delight in them.
I lied, I never had a lacquered table or a summit.
And there's no time left for wrapping my muscles
around a dead egg.

El geco de Calvino

No podría definir al lagarto pequeño
en el fondo del tronco.
Nudos de otro árbol inalcanzable
y parapetos antiguos lo extravían
(oquedades legítimas).
Era un pequeño lagarto gris
—ese que viera el señor Palomar antes de morir.
O aquel de los falsos aretes
que asustaron para siempre los lóbulos de mi madre.
Estuvo quieto mirándome de soslayo,
sin cruzar la obsesión reflejada en sus patas.

Color triste de tronco semipodrido y sin luz
es un obsequio caro de la tarde en la plaza.
Le tiro bolitas de papel endurecidas, hojuelas de maíz,
y el sismo no logra entristecerlo aún más.
La reverberación hace su cola algo más clara,
más frágil.
La nube filtra un tiempo que se va en los dos
a oscurecer entre las ramas.
(Ha visto el horror de mi rostro, el desplome.)
Se irá cuando enciendan las luces artificiales
entre el ajetreo de los turistas y los niños al volver.
El lagarto ha soñado ser hombre
y corre entre las raíces secas de mis falanges,
por la mente común que nos envuelve.
Se enrosca al tronco viejo y musgoso,
y mientras traga una mariposa de alambre
caída (ingenuamente) de su ala en mi brazo,
lo atrapo.

Calvino's gecko

I couldn't give definition to the tiny lizard
in the tree's hollow.
Knots from another unreachable tree
and ancient barricades sent him astray
(genuine cavities).
He was a tiny gray lizard
—the one Mr. Palomar saw as he died.
Or the lizard from the clip-on earrings
that forever terrorized my mother's lobes.
He was calm, watching me out of the corner of his eye,
never crossing the fixation bouncing off his feet.

The sad color of a half-rotted trunk, lightless,
he's an extravagant gift from evening in the plaza.
I toss him hard little balls of paper and cornflakes.
The shock wave doesn't make him any sadder.
Its reverberation somehow makes his tail more visible,
more fragile.
The cloud filters time moving away in both of them
to fall dark between the branches.
(He has seen the horror of my face, its collapse.)
He'll leave when electric lights flick on
with the bustle of tourists going out and children coming back.
This lizard dreamed about being a man
and runs between the dry roots of my phalanges,
through the communal mind enveloping us.
He twists around the old mossy trunk
and as he swallows a wire butterfly
fallen (ingenuously) from the wing onto my arm,
I trap him.

El último sello

Jugábamos a las películas.
Era de madrugada.
Oía risas y recordaba
otras películas.
El hombro al que me recosté
en el cine de barrio.
La copia como siempre era mala
y los de arriba chiflaban ante la imprecisión
de otra imagen cortada sobre un cuerpo
amputado por el proyeccionista.
Él jugaba su partida de ajedrez...
con la última pieza escondida
entre la muerte y tú.
La muerte era entonces esa vida miserable
que afuera te esperaba
(y engañándola)
te escondías para ser proyectada desde
"la luz más crepuscular que existe" —decías.
Pensando que nadie estaba viendo del otro lado del set
un cuerpo roto en miles de partículas por el aire.
Tu sumisión o el vejado perfil.

The Final Seal

We were acting out film scenes.
It was early morning.
I'd hear laughter and remember
other films.
The man I'd lean against
in the neighborhood theater.
As always it was a poor reproduction
and people above whistled disapproval
when an extra image appeared, cut over a body
amputated by the projectionist.
He was playing his game of chess…
its final piece hidden
between death and you.
At that time death was the miserable life
waiting for you outside
(and deceiving her).
You hid in order to be projected through
"the most twilit light there is" —your words.
Thinking that no one from the other side of the set was
watching
a body smashed into thousands of particles by the air.
Your surrender or humiliated profile.

Barrio Chino

Cine de medianoche rayando la pantalla
con su copia de reproducciones
ya en desuso.
Tú venías desde el embarcadero siguiendo la Alameda
y la neblina era humo de un cigarro
a medio apagar, a medio encender.
El presupuesto de algo vivo a tu lado,
una colilla.
Cuando creyéndote Mónica Viti con esas grandes tetas
(que te pertenecían sólo por un momento)
aproximaban el gran escote rojo de la llama
a los espectadores
y cogías terror
de que te crecieran a ese tamaño sobrenatural
las tuyas.

Hoy la mente ha confundido muchas escenas
y concentrado sólo algunas.
Podías hacer una sola proyección,
con el material acumulado por los años.
Una hilera de amigos que iban contigo,
ya no están.
No entran sin pagar con sus falsos carnets de estudiantes.
La crédula acomodadora sonreía ante las mismas caras
de un original que en la foto
nunca se correspondía
—la foto de esa artista que luego pretendías ser
en otra parte mutilada del filme.
"Tanta ridiculez, llegar a la oscuridad
para sellar el rastro de una imagen perdida!"

Chinatown

Midnight theater scratching up the screen
with its copy of reproductions
already obsolete.
You'd come from the harbor along the Alameda
and the fog was smoke from a cigarette
half-out, half-lit.
The premise of something living at your side,
its stub.
When imagining you to be Monica Vitti with her enormous
                                                                    boobs
(which belonged to you for just one instant)
they'd move the great red cleavage of the flame
toward spectators
and suddenly you'd be terrified
that yours
would balloon to that supernatural size.

Today the mind blends several scenes
and brings certain ones into focus.
You could create a single projection
from material accumulated over the years.
A line of friends who used to go with you
but aren't here anymore.
They don't get in without paying, with fake student IDs.
The gullible woman selling tickets would smile
at the same faces, which never matched
the original in the photo
—a photo of the artist you would later try to be
in a different, mutilated panel of the film.
"Ridiculous, going into the dark
to hunt for the outline of some lost image!"

"...Bichito de la oscuridad y el frío..."
—decía tu padre,
el único ser que siempre supo hallarte
reclinada en el espacio sin lugar
de una butaca hundiéndose
en el escote de la Viti.
Lugar perfecto para ti (y para él).
Sitio que ha dejado de ser un lugar,
un límite preciso en la imposibilidad del sitio
donde vuelves a recostar tu cabeza
entre rollos develados por una realidad que los venció.
Y donde esperas, "con paciencia infinita",
la escena final.

"Creature of dark and cold,"
your father would say,
the only one who could always figure out where you were:
reclining in the placeless space
of a theater seat, sinking
into Vitti's cleavage.
The perfect place for you (and him).
Location that left off being a place,
a specific limit on the incapacity of the site
where you rest your head again
among reels exposed by a reality defeating them.
And where you wait, "with infinite patience," for
the final scene.

La palabra jarra

para J. M.

Te autorizo a sentir la palabra jarra.
"Cómo es posible que jarra no significara jarra"
—dice el niño de cuatro años— y nos da la advertencia:
el texto engaña con sonido de metal
para materiales diversos
que pueden ser cristal, plástico o lata.
La palabra jarra sostiene una arbitrariedad de la especie
de esas palabras que trastornan la ilusión de aquel niño
que esperaba sonar las diferentes hablas;
también modos de agarrar, de poseer un objeto y más tarde,
algún ordenamiento artificial.
Por eso, al crecer, escribe otra cosa por jarra,
otra cosa por destino, y se hace escritor
para corromper la supuesta facticidad de una vida,
para matar ciertas lógicas.
Y la palabra deja de ser algo material,
toma la velocidad de un tren que se descarga,
la locura ciega de su locomotora, el silbido
de esos rostros desvencijados que han pasado por él
a través del paisaje otoñal de la ventanilla:
rostros, animales y árboles amarillos
haciendo el mohín de alguna cosa que aún representan
sin claridad.

Vuelve a tocar la palabra en recorrido
y el mismo tren de regreso despedaza la imagen,
despedaza el porvenir que se repite
por compases largos, largos, largos,
atravesados por siglos del uso que la vence.

The word *pitcher*

for J. M.

I authorize you to perceive the word *pitcher.*
"How come *pitcher* doesn't mean *pitcher*,"
asks the four-year-old, and he gives us warning:
text deceives with metallic noise
for different substances, maybe
glass, plastic, or tin.
The word *pitcher* maintains an arbitrariness like
those words that upset the illusions of the child
who expected to sound out different sorts of speech,
different modes for grasping, possessing an object and later
some artificial way to create order.
So as he ages he writes some other thing for *pitcher*,
some other thing for destiny, and he becomes a writer
to corrupt the supposed facticity of a life,
to kill off certain forms of logic.
The word leaves off being something material.
It takes on the velocity of a train without cargo,
the blind insanity of its engine, the whistle
of those rickety faces passing through him
by way of the window's autumnal landscape:
faces, animals, yellow trees
grimacing something they still represent
confusedly.

He touches the word again en route
and the same train, returning, shatters the image,
shatters the future that repeats
across lengthy, lengthy, lengthy measures,
crossing over centuries of customary usage that overpower the
                                                            image.

Y cuando toma el líquido que al fin ha echado
en aquel recipiente que no se atreve a nombrar,
con su mano llagada, pequeña y temblorosa,
lo ve impuro, turbio, balancearse contra el fondo,
y ya no está contenido, ya no es real,
ya no lo ve.
Se ve solo él, agachado, mirándose contra el tiempo
del líquido.

Entonces cacharrea la palabra justificación
y la palabra jarra vuelve a ser olvidada,
desgarrada por una sensación de vacío
contra el asa de hierro por donde él ha iniciado el proceso
de verter —en descarrilamiento, los orígenes—
los tristes zumos de la inspiración, las antiguas
voces ordenadas por alguna ley que no comprende aún,
y tira el líquido disperso
con violencia
al suelo.

Es cuando la palabra jarra se desvanece
para quedar fingidamente inscrita y
superpuesta en la obsesión de unos dedos
que por un momento
la sostuvo.

He drinks liquid and expels it
with his small, trembling, wounded hand
into a receptacle better left unnamed.
He sees that it's impure, turbid, balancing against the bottom,
it's no longer contained, no longer real,
he no longer sees it.
You only see him, bent over, staring at his face in the rhythm
of the liquid.

Then he crushes the word *justification*
and the word *pitcher* is forgotten,
smashed by the sensation of emptiness,
against the iron handle he had used to initiate the process
of pouring out sad inspirational juices, ancient
voices ordered by some law he still doesn't comprehend
—emptied by derailment, origins—
and he throws the disordered liquid
violently
to the ground.

It's when the word *pitcher* dissipates
that its fiction is inscribed and
superimposed in the obsession of fingers
that had momentarily
upheld the word.

Lámpara de Julio

para Julio Ramos

Estrenamos tu lámpara de papel de arroz
y batalla la llama más antigua sus conquistas.
El viento del verano forcejea contra el pálido azul
indeciso
al subir, al bajar.
Huele a papel de arroz en la noche
y sostengo la última llamarada de la razón
contra el papel quemado.

Es la lámpara de Julio (sin piedad)
zarza seca de humo
cada frase adquirida en la cosecha.
Recupero sobre el papel caliente, granos enfermos
y otros amarillos,
como si la gravedad de su luz tranquila (arriba),
más verdinegra al fondo
fuera tu pasado
que se acerca a mi mano
y contorsiona entre semillas
el devenir de un baile al fondo.

Entonces, puedo ver siluetas lujuriosas,
andamios. Todo lo que no viví.
Encima de la llama un claro.
En el corazón del claro,
otra mano rojiza agazapada:
humo arriba y perdición abajo.
Esa mano, entre trozos de papel escurridizos,
me indica un mapa del destino inalcanzable.
Parece que termina, se apaga

Julio's lamp

for Julio Ramos

For the first time we light your rice paper lamp
and the most ancient flame wrestles with its conquests.
A summer breeze struggles against its pale blue,
indecisive,
rising and falling.
The night smells like rice paper
and I grasp the last burst of reason
flaring against burnt paper.

It's Julio's lamp (merciless),
dry bramble of smoke,
each phrase acquired from harvest time.
I use the hot paper to cup grains, some diseased
and others yellowed
as though the severity of its calm light (from above),
a darker background green,
were your past
approaching my hand,
which wrings out among seeds the
evolution of a background dance.

Then I can see lustful silhouettes,
scaffoldings. Everything I never experienced.
An interval of clarity above the flame.
Tensed at its center,
another reddened hand:
smoke above, perdition below.
Between elusive bits of paper, that hand
points me toward a map for an unreachable fate.
It seems to end, to blink out

(que flota por la inercia desprendida)
y ya no volverá a encender su espiga ¡tan alta!
si amanece entre las sombras
olor crudo
en mi lámpara.

4 de julio de 2000

(floating open, on inertia)
and it will no longer light that spike, so high up!
if among the shadows
a harsh odor awakens
inside my lamp.

July 4, 2000

Zigzags

"*Todo remata en el gris*" —*ha dicho el pintor.*
Parcelas de azul y claroscuro.
Densidad de un malestar naranja a contrapelo.
Todo remata (definitivamente)
en el círculo gris
y se vuelve a mover como gelatina que flota
enfrentándose a un espacio de creación amarillo.
Un espacio de norma mediática.

Los colores penetran mis órganos.
Bajan, suben, se arrastran
y trastean impacientes
el carrusel donde la sangre juega
en su orgía perpetua.
Concentrados, fluidos ante la mísera realidad,
toman un valor de presencia.
"Está en mí …transparente."
"Está en ti."
El color, en el cual volabas hasta la casa
donde estaba el Comienzo…

Al despertar, todo era violeta
—gelatina de los sueños cuarteados por un reflejo.
"No podemos hacer más —dices—
que soñar este espíritu del color que vemos
(o que creemos ver)
junto a un espacio permanente."
"Entonces, ¿no hay libertad?" —pregunto.

"La libertad se mueve en fuga perpetua
de un trabajo de luz
y nos hace perdernos de algún lugar preciso.

Zigzags

"Everything is finished in gray"—said the painter.
Fields of blue, chiaroscuro.
Density of orange unrest working against the grain.
Everything finishes (definitively)
inside the gray circle
and resumes its motion, floating like gelatin
in front of a space of yellow creation.
A space norming the medium.

Colors invade my organs.
They fall, rise, drag
and rummage around, impatient,
in the carousel where blood plays
in endless orgy.
Concentrated, fluid in the face of impoverished reality,
they take on the value of presence.
"It is in me ...transparent."
"It is in you."
The color on which you flew toward the house
where the Beginning could be found...

Upon awakening, everything was violet
—jelly dreams, divided by reflection.
"We can do no more," say you,
"than dream the spirit of this color we see
(or think we see)
next to a permanent space."
"So: there is no freedom?" I ask.

"Freedom takes perpetual flight
from a lightwork
and disorients us from any specific location.

Aunque las fugas se opongan
y establezcan contradicciones
sobre ella" —respondes.

"Entonces, ¿no hay color?"

Though its flights may clash,
establishing contradictions
over it," you respond.

"So: there is no color?"

La ley en Sainte-Victoire

Ese hombre con una cuchara sobre el papel
dibujó dos cumbres.
"Hay que subirlas" —dijo, señalando hacia el cielo.
No sabía por qué
aquellas montañas con sus declinaciones
lo perseguían, retándolo.
Algunos lo siguieron
desde la parte más baja (y degradada) de la cumbre
donde se había propagado un sentimiento de caer,
han vuelto a empinarse
sobre la roca de un blanco calcinado
y musgo...

Los movimientos de la cuchara en el aire
(aleteando plata)
son los esfuerzos por llegar
a alguna certidumbre.
Aunque no puedan ver
lo que está detrás de la pendiente
ni alcanzarlo jamás
continúan.
Una brizna echándose a perder...
Aunque lo asuman
y sepan que no llegarán,
que no pueden alcanzarlo,
lo intentarán
confiados.

Como un cuadro inconcluso
que al pasar nadie ve
y en un descuido del pintor
el deseo flotara sobre

The law in Sainte-Victoire

That man drew two peaks on the paper
with a spoon.
"They must be climbed," he said, gesturing toward the sky.
He didn't know why
those mountains and their declinations
chased him, challenging him.
Some pursued him
from the lowest (most degraded) part of the summit
where a feeling of falling had spread;
they're up on tiptoe again
over the rock's sunbaked white
and moss...

The spoon's motions in the air
(silver flapping)
are efforts to arrive
at certainty of fact.
Though they may not be able to see
what's beyond the slope,
may never get there,
they go on.
A blade of grass destroyed...
They may come to terms with it,
know they won't get there,
that they can't reach it,
yet they'll try,
confident.

Like an unfinished painting
that no one notices while passing by.
And due to an oversight by the painter
desire floats over

los peñascos,
"pasta de polvo seca a paletadas breves",
encima
está la cúspide.

Habíamos llegado por casualidad
a través de los desvíos de una curva
una trampa (su mente).
Detrás de la mesa de la antigua fonda medieval
sobre un mantel extendido ante nosotros,
la profundidad quemada
nos mantenía vivos.
La descubrimos por el miedo a perderla
al borde
(esa fragilidad que da la pertenencia),
desconfiamos de sus flores naranjas,
de la voluptuosidad de su contorno,
del paisaje que, al tener frente a nosotros,
¡tan confiados!
nos vence.

the outcrops,
"paste from dry dust, in quick tosses,"
the pinnacle
above.

We arrived by chance
through the detours from a curve:
a trap (his mind).
At a table in the cheap old restaurant, medieval cuisine
set before us on a tablecloth,
a charred profundity
kept us alive.
We discovered it through the fear of its loss,
at the brink
(fragility, which grants belonging),
we distrust its orange flowers,
the voluptuousness of its outline,
the landscape appearing before us
—so confident! we
are vanquished by it.

Amatista

Él era algo más alto, atlético.
Corría las pistas con frenesí.
Cola de caballo otra vez enlazada por el rojo azafrán.
Ya sólo tengo esa memoria usada
de un tocadiscos Motorola,
fuente de placer el rock and roll *(obsesivo),*
la aguja de diamante cortada con prisa
y la placa negra una y mil veces
hasta enloquecer.
Lanzada otra vez por debajo de sus piernas,
grito, gritar, gritando...
Era la primera en el baile y la primera en todo
(en la clase de ballet, jota por nada).
El arco del brazo exacto de la pubertad.
Pero él seguía más alto, inalcanzable.
Aunque bailara en punta,
aunque sonara doble jota aragonesa.
No llegaba a sus pies con la cola vencida.
No era mi piedra la amatista, no
—era por no ser, la más falsa—,
la fuente morada de toda declinación o
protuberancia fácil.
Corría delante y se jactaba
(yo, jadeante),
no lo pude alcanzar ni sostener
con escaramuzas
en el disco, en la saya,
sobre un anillo de metal barato.

Amethyst

He was a bit taller, athletic.
Passionate about his racing.
The horse's tail tied with red saffron again.
Now the only thing I have left is this secondhand memory
of a Motorola record player,
our source of (obsessive) rock-and-roll pleasures,
the diamond needle cutting quickly
and the black disc, a thousand and one times
to the brink of insanity.
Swept between his legs again
I shout, to shout, shouting...
I was the best at dance and the best in everything
(a jota in dance class, for nothing).
The precise arc of the arm during puberty.
But he was still taller, unreachable.
Even if I danced on pointe or
clicked an Aragonese double jota with castanets.
Defeated, I couldn't get to his feet.
The amethyst was not my stone, no
—it was about nonbeing, the fakest—
purple source of all declination or
an easy projection.
He ran ahead and boasted
(me, panting)
I couldn't reach him or keep up
with my forays
across the record, across my skirt,
across my cheap metal ring.

Baldositas

Las noches de enero son muy frías,
pero al pesar del clima
caminábamos contra esa frialdad
apretados del brazo.
Subíamos la cuesta
y ya no volvería a caer aquella nieve fina
sobre la estatua de Pushkin,
ni estarían repletas las estaciones del metro.

He despegado otra loza sin querer
—piedra de mi muslo—, esta mesa de azulejos ostenta
sus desprendimientos.
Así la hicimos, así, para que al desprenderse
saltaran con la respiración, al humo,
mis alucinaciones.

Noche de enero, bre-ví-si-ma.
La estrella polar como brújula en el cielo de la mesa,
su atrevida luz que asoma si abro la ventana
distante.
Se ha despegado del espacio roto
con su infinita manera de volver, cayendo,
ahora quemando mi muslo
otra frialdad.

Ella estaba escondida
en la nostalgia de quien creíamos ser entonces.
Demasiada inmediata realidad.
Al tocar esta piedra sólo yo,
—y con mucho trabajo—
logro distinguir
qué color aparece.

Glazed tiles

The January nights are icy,
but in spite of the weather
we were walking into the cold
arm in arm.
We were climbing a slope
and that fine snow wouldn't fall any longer
on Pushkin's statue,
the metro stations wouldn't fill.

I accidentally knocked out another ceramic bit
—stone from my thigh—this tiled table flaunts
its lost objects.
That's how we made it, so that when they came loose
they would skip out with our breath, with trails of smoke,
my delusions.

A night in January, so very brief.
North Star like a compass on the table of the sky,
its cheeky light winking if I open the window,
far off.
It chipped away from the broken part
with its infinite form of return, falling,
now burning my thigh
with a different kind of cold.

She was hidden
inside the nostalgia about people we once believed ourselves to be.
Reality: too immediate.
Touching this stone only I
can make out
—and with a lot of effort—
which color surfaces.

Tibio, macizo, prieto...
No recuerdo si es mía o alguna vez fingió
esa posesión que distingue su apariencia del resto.

Época extraña dilatándose
al despegarse después
completamente.

Lukewarm, solid, dark…
Mine? I can't remember—maybe a possession she once faked,
to distinguish one appearance from the rest.

A strange time, dilating
and later it was knocked out
completely.

Qué decir...

Qué decir de este día,
del tamaño vasto y reforzado del día
tan azul como una piscina abierta
que me invita en febrero a la demencia?
Qué decir del trazo de tu pulgar sobre mi vena
también azulada?
Alimentos terribles,
necesarios.

La brisa de la ciudad pegajosa.
La voz corrompida por el griterío
y una mala palabra justo al centro de esta
salvaje soledad contaminada
que vuelve hacia mí (tardíamente)
sus restos.
Podría morir de intensidad sostenida.
Lo traigo en el bultico diario
amarrado a la cintura,
sujeto al palo de madera (de la memoria)
con una horqueta pequeña.
Allí, lo engancho.

Este de hoy, único,
azul de febrero inoxidable,
conchitas de azúcar prieta
y carapachos de recuerdos rotos.
Su intensidad me hace enloquecer
presa de una pasión sin límites.
¡Lo deseaba tanto
que me volví de espaldas con indiferencia
y corrí las ventanas!

What is there to say...

What is there to say about this day,
about the vast bulwarked size of the day
blue as a pool open to the February sky
inviting me inside dementia?
What is there to say about your thumb's path
across my vein, another shade of blue?
Forms of sustenance, terrible and
necessary.

Breeze from the sticky city.
The voice corrupted with uproar
and a curse word right at the center of
this wild contaminated solitude
that turns its remains (too late)
on me.
I could die of this protracted intensity.
I carry it in a daypack
strapped to my waist,
pegged to the stick of wood (memory)
with a little fork.
I hook it in there.

This one, today, unique,
February's rustproof blue,
brown sugar shells
and broken-memory carapace.
Its intensity drives me mad,
prisoner of a limitless passion.
Something I desired so much
that I turned my back in indifference
and drew my curtains!

Sellé los huecos para no verlo aparecer
contra la claridad
(era amargo volver deshilachada).
Correr hacia la diminuta hormiga
que me ha visto tantas veces mentir
envenenándola
sobre el mismo plato
de la prisión cotidiana.
Era ingrato.
No quise que me viera así.

Conservo su dolor y lo convierto en otra cosa.
Lo trazo con un compás sobre el mar.
Lo pinto con palabras que no pronuncié mientras callaba.
Cualquier poder ejerce una convicción brutal sobre él.
Lo deposito en la postal, cerrada.
Lo fundo al cartón para que no vuelva
a representar su mascarada frente a mí
y, luego,
escapa.

I sealed all the holes so as not to see it appear
against the clarity
(so bitter, to return all frayed).
Running toward the diminutive ant
who has seen me lie so many times
poisoning her
with the same plate
in my everyday prison.
The day was ungrateful.
Once I didn't want it to see me like that.

I keep its sorrow and transform it into something else.
Trace it with a compass over the sea.
Paint it with words that I didn't say when I stayed silent.
Any power inflicts a brutal conviction on it.
I place it on a postcard, closed.
Put it inside a cardboard box so it won't restage
a masquerade for me
but then
it gets away.

El recorrido de la araña

Cómo creció hasta esconderse
detrás de un oso rojo de peluche, la vida?
Adquirió una dimensión de patas largas
condenándose contra la pared,
y al final, un tejido.
La disciplina férrea de seguir sin retroceder.
Cuántas cosas comparten contigo
los oscuros huecos de esta casa?
El cristal aflojando ciertos tramos
y la cúspide hacia el despertar
que no es montaña
ni elevación tan plana,
que al enredar ciertos hilos a un trayecto
ata de otro tan frágil
(y superfluo)
contra el cristal de la ventana,
mi vejez.

The spider's path

Life—how did it grow and hide
behind a red teddy bear?
It developed a long-legged dimension,
damned against the wall,
with a web at the end.
The iron discipline of going forward, no retreat.
How many things do they share with you,
the dark holes around this house?
The glass giving way to certain distortions
and the apex near awakening
which is neither a mountain
nor such a flat plateau;
as it tangles certain threads into a trajectory
it loops one more of them in, so fragile
(and superfluous)
against the window glass:
my old age.

A un nido de golondrina azul

para Alejandro Häsler

Nido de bambúes que recorriste
(trazo sobre trazo)
con nudos en sus extremos
para llegar al terreno del ave que puso allí
su necesidad de estar apaciguada.
De aquella golondrina que antes se fue
y ahora regresó al mismo sitio
donde partió al invierno,
sobre una fuente de mar arrebujada
(como cada ave y su corazoncito en la partida).

La misma flecha sur como un hilo de savia.
Y yo, no sé por qué te veo subir, subir,
entre las trampas del bambú por el alero
tomando por la retaguardia hacia un abismo
y sus declinaciones.
Y ya no será nada caer o salvarse
si la frase ha vuelto con exactitud
a remover un nido vacío
que se desprenderá,
una añoranza.

Tomo un pedazo de soga y no defino bien si se llegó.
Tú, el lazo endurecido de la alternativa contraria.
"Pero, ¿llegamos?" —dices.

La arremetida contra el nido es locura que pica en la cabeza.
Gramos de un sol, abajo.
Cuentagotas de rocío

To a blue swallow's nest

Bamboo nest that you laid out
(line over line)
knots at the ends
to access the territory of a bird who laid
its need to be calmed there.
The territory of a swallow who left before
then came back to the same place
where it set off for winter,
huddled above a tidepool
(like every bird, its little heart, departing).

Same arrow, southern as a thread of sap.
And me, I don't know why I see you climb, climb
among bamboo snares, along the eaves,
taking the back way toward an abyss
and its drop-offs.
And it will mean nothing to fall or to save yourself
if the sentence has excised
an empty nest again
which will detach,
a longing.

I pick a piece of rope and can't tell whether it was long enough to
reach.
You, a hardened cord of contrary alternative.
"But do we get there?" you say.

The assault on the nest is insanity pricking inside your head.
Grams of sun, below.
Droppers with dew

por donde se fuga en vuelo ágil
(a derecha, izquierda)
sin medir la capacidad de sus bandazos
a la cuerda de bambúes,
¡tan frágil!
que al fingir la resistencia del extremo anudado,
el otro se revienta de mi parte.
¿Aguantarás?
¿Resisto?

through which one pitches in agile flight
(right, left)
without measuring the power from swerves
along the bamboo cord,
so fragile
that with resistance from the knotted side,
the other one on my side falls apart.
Will you hold up?
Will I hold out?

Mi pequeño libro

El libro de Marina a mis pies ha caído.
(La artista y el poder)
y el libro abierto,
"Mi Pushkin" en el suelo.
Sus pequeños ojos escrutando
alguna infiltración, aquella voz, otro lenguaje.
No comprende de dónde ha salido esa queja
y quiere reconocerse en ella también.
Los demás han desaparecido en la partida.
"Atención, baja un peldaño hacia atrás,
recógete." Es la orden que da el libro
desde el suelo.

El libro que habla deshojado,
un tronco vivo, pero muerto.
Un tronco que me quema.
No hay voz que apague su grito desde el suelo,
aunque pretendo mezclarla con la mía,
un susurro contra ese grito de ella,
ya no puedo.
Le beso la mejilla. Siento una cal cosmética
de primera calidad, un polvo milenario
que me empolva los labios.
No quiero convencerlo.

El triángulo lo forman las dos figuras trazadas con la regla.
Rígido buda de imitación de jade.
Pequeña artista (miniatura de porcelana hueso)
y el libro de ella caído contra el suelo.
Le beso la mejilla a sabiendas
de que beso con ingratitud
y recojo el polvo revuelto por la alfombra con mi beso.

My little book

Marina's book has fallen at my feet.
(The artist and power)
and the open book,
My Pushkin on the floor.
Its little eyes scrutinizing
an infiltration, that distant voice, another language.
It doesn't understand where the moan came from
but wants to find itself in the sound.
Others disappeared with the departure.
"Attention: go back down one step,
pull yourself together." An order given by the book
from the floor.

The book speaking without pages, leafless;
a trunk both living and dead.
A log: it burns me.
No voice can drown her shout from the floor
even when I try to merge it with my own,
a murmur against its shout,
I can't do it.
I kiss its cheek. I notice powder, a luxury
cosmetic, an age-old dusting
left on my lips.
I don't want to make him believe.

The triangle is made by two figures, sketched with a ruler.
Rigid imitation-jade Buddha.
Little artist (a miniature in bone china)
and her book fallen on the floor.
I kiss her cheek knowing full well
that I'm kissing it with ingratitude
and with my kiss I pick up the powder scattered across the floor.

"Este será mi último encuentro" —prometo.
Todavía creo que el mal
puede volverse de repente algún bien
con la cercanía de mi boca en la página
(mi boca que succiona los arrepentimientos).
Recojo el libro (o alguien lo recoge).
Quiero explicarle quién fue ella,
pero ya no hay tiempo para hacer el bien,
para reconciliarnos.
La reflexión del mal es apoderarse del poco bien que queda
y someterlo.
Aprieto más el libro.
Una membrana viva sobre el pecho.
Un cataplasma hirviendo
con residuos de impotencia
que no me absuelven por la irresponsabilidad cometida.
Sé que respira, su dolor, el libro. Ella...

Quiero explicarte
cómo suceden estas cosas.
Un gesto vago que no comprenderás.
La rabia interna contra la mayoría que contempla
enardecida.
Siento todo lo que la muerte amenaza:
los dientes inferiores mordiendo la palabra
de los que no aceptan la verdad.
Esa sospecha por la osadía de haberme acercado
al pedestal de melopea.

Bajo de nuevo el compás y pincho,
con su punta afilada y mohosa,
mi carne contra el libro.
El libro tiembla
y el triángulo se deshace.

"This will be my last meeting," I promise.
I still believe that evil
can suddenly turn to good
with my mouth on the page
(my mouth soaks up remorse).
I pick up the book (or someone else does).
I want to tell him who she was,
but there's no left time for doing the good deed,
for reconciliation.

Reflecting on evil means finding the little bit of good that remains
and taking control of it.
I squeeze the book harder.
A living membrane against my chest.
A boiling poultice
with residues of impotence
that won't absolve me for my irresponsible act.
I know the book is breathing, know its pain. She…

I want to tell you
how these things happen.
It's an unclear gesture that you won't understand.
The internal rage against a majority that passes judgment,
                                                    whipped up.
I sense death threatening every thing:
lower teeth biting the word off
from those who refuse to accept truth.
Their suspicion about my audacity, having approached
the grand pedestal with a poetic chant.

With my downbeat I cut my skin
on the book, its
biting and moldy edge.
The book quivers
and the triangle breaks apart.

Salgo por la puerta trasera al espectáculo
traspasando otras combinaciones.
He besado su mejilla encerada
—límite imperdonable de la mirada
siempre sujeta a un fin.

Nunca lo podré olvidar.
Fue mi culpa.
Marina no escapará del texto
y morirá encerrada.

I go out through the back door, into the spectacle,
past other combinations.
I kissed her polished cheek
—unpardonable boundary put upon the gaze,
always subject to an ending.

I'll never be able to forget it.
It was my fault.
Marina will not escape from the text.
She'll die shut inside it.

La casa de St. Ives

Para V. y V.

La negra mariposa tras la puerta amenaza.
Sobrevuela mi cama otra vez.
Afiladas, sus alas prietas
como punzones a mi alrededor
traen su danza macabra.
En la ventana, un faltante número sesenta y seis
ha decorado mi mente
y la devora.

Recuerdo la casa de St. Ives donde ellas
guardaban mariposas funestas
con la obsesión de sobrevolar una vez más
hacia el atardecer.
Dos hermanas que prendieron de su ala absurda
—el incesto y la fama— con un alfiler de la ventana,
hoy decorada con ribetes falsos
de aquella tempestad victoriana.

Pero llegó el día
en que se quebró la membrana sucia del amanecer
y los faltantes en las cuentas del padre.
Nació un hijo en el agua encharcada de la habitación.
En medio del silencio, "¿ ...qué tul poner sobre la cama
para que no regrese la negra mariposa de antaño
a enturbiar el ojo pardo de mi hija
y haya que sacrificar todos los cuadros
en la antigua hoguera?"

Una voz llega desde la verja (que por suerte)
aún nos separa.

Her house at St. Ives

for V. and V.

Behind the door, the black butterfly threatens.
It's flying over my bed again.
Its dusky wings, filed like burins,
lift in macabre dance
around me.
In the window, a sixty-six missing from its wing
embellishes my mind
and consumes her.

I remember the house at St. Ives where the girls
kept baleful butterflies,
fixated on flying overhead
toward the setting sun once more.
Two sisters who pinned ridiculous wings
—incest, a reputation—at a window,
one decorated today with the false trimmings
from a Victorian tempest.

But the day came
when dawn's dirty membrane broke open,
along with gaps in her father's accounting books.
In one room, a son was born into a pool of water.
Through the silence: "Which tulle should I hang over the bed
so the black butterfly won't return out of the past
to darken my daughter's brown eye
and force the sacrifice of all paintings
to an ancient bonfire?"

A voice arrives from the iron gate that (fortunately)
still separates us.

135

Donde había pasado los veranos de su infancia
recostada a esa frágil división
hecha de la fama necesaria, ahora hay pasto.
Y las hormigas suben,
arrasan unos edredones enchumbados con sangre
(bajo la niebla insuficiente, pero persistente)
que cubre los faltantes
contra la verja de entrada
permanentemente cerrada.

¿Fue su virginidad vencida de once años
fermentada a los cuarenta y ocho,
forzada a los sesenta y seis,
que vuelve a ser
un aleteo de muerte
y de poder?

Allí estaba su padre tumbando libros viejos
al precipicio del entresuelo.
Viejo sótano donde caen mujeres suicidas, follajes
(cosas turbias que ahora no recuerda bien).
Cuerpos de mariposas gigantes
bajo el techo de St. Ives que lo resiste todo:
hasta un detalle de ala tatuada, pero insípida
entre otras suspicacias
de viejo corazón petrificado junto a una lápida
donde ahora vive,
pez de piedra verde,
viejo animal, mi padre,
el de ellas.

El retorno de ese vuelo inseguro trae
cierta frase de mi hija: "…la mariposa ha muerto
y se engurruña sobre sí misma, furiosa,
en la esquina que obtuvo en la ventana…"

Now, where she once spent her childhood summers
leaning against the fragile divide
made out of the need for reputation, there is hay.
And ants climb,
dragging bloody eiderdowns
(under an inadequate but persistent fog)
blanketing absences
at the entrance, gated and
permanently closed.

Was it her virginity, taken at age eleven,
fermented at forty-eight,
forced at sixty-six,
that again becomes
a fluttering of death
and power?

There was her father knocking old books
into the steep drop-off under the mezzanine.
An old basement where suicidal women fall, verbiage
(clouded things I can't remember clearly now).
Bodies of enormous butterflies
under the roof of St. Ives, which endures it all:
down to a detail on a tattooed wing, but insipid
among other suspicions
inside an old heart now turned to stone
next to the grave marker where he lives,
a fish in green stone,
an old animal, my father,
theirs.

Its uncertain return flight elicits
a statement from my daughter: "…the butterfly died
and it's feeling bad for itself, it's angry,
in that corner it got in the window…"

"Tatagua —musito una y otra vez—, Tatagua",
muerta de incertidumbre
esta mañana.

"*Tatagua*," I mutter over and over, "black butterfly,"
dead of perplexity
this morning.

Carretera

Largo atraviesas el crepúsculo, un preámbulo.
(Él, al volante).
La carretera es una pauta abierta
donde la secuencia es antes que forma
luz.
Al prenderse los semáforos
el cielo es blanco
y los árboles arrastran con el viento
sombras oscurecidas de otros árboles.

Ahora ves el pentagrama de una vida,
ese sitio de intersección volátil.
Dónde está el límite de este atardecer de hoy
y luego el de mañana?
En qué momento muere con exactitud la tarde?
En qué momento decae, o despierta?
Cómo se pierde el color, o la negrura azul?
Cómo aparece por detrás de los árboles, de las casas,
y frente a ti?
Aparece? Desaparece?
Está, o se perdió sin ser?

El chofer sigue la marcha por el cono de luz artificial
que le corresponde a su linealidad.
Tú desvías el cauce original de su música
y atraviesas la causalidad mutua de un tiempo que se va,
dentro de ti, a perder,
sin saber del que viene.

Entonces,
juegas al pon desde la acera contraria
cuando ves la figura del auto que atraviesa la tarde

Freeway

Tempo: largo. You're moving through sunset, a preamble.
(He's at the wheel.)
The freeway is a wide-open musical staff
where sequence exists before light
takes shape.
When the lights flick on
the sky is white
and trees use the wind to tug at
darkening shadows of other trees.

Now you see the five-line stave of one lifetime,
that site of volatile intersection.
Where is the boundary of today's twilight?
of the one coming tomorrow?
At what moment, exactly, does the evening die?
At what moment does it flag or revive?
How does color disappear, or the deep blue dark?
How does it appear behind trees, houses,
in front of you?
Does it appear? Disappear?
Is it there or did it vanish without coming to be?

The driver follows the course set by a cone of artificial light
that corresponds to his linearity.
You divert the original flow of his music
and cross on the mutual causality of a tempo that goes away,
inside you, vanishing
with no sense of the one to come next.

Then
you hopscotch down the opposing sidewalk
and see the figure of a car as it moves through evening

"junto al bloque de niebla del océano" —has dicho.
Te ves, tantos años después, tantos años antes,
en el nunca regreso.
Pero la sabiduría del cuerpo extraña al límite,
renuncia a la distancia.
El aquí que lo confronta es siempre el mismo: un hiato perfecto.

Saludas a la que se va, a la que parte. Los semáforos
siguen verdes, anaranjados o escurridizos.
La tarde es reducida a una espera que se transita, un borde fibroso
que acaricias con el dedo sobre el parabrisas, húmedo al fin.
El dedo es el sitio que siente la llovizna.
Y la llovizna, como una tela transparente, oculta los dos tiempos,
la textura definitiva con que está hecha la realidad,
su telón.

"by the block of ocean fog," to borrow your words.
You see yourself so many years later, so many earlier,
in the noneturn.
But the body's wisdom misses the boundary.
It renounces distance.
The here confronting it is always the same: a perfect hiatus.

You greet the woman leaving, the one moving away. Traffic
lights
go on being green, amber, or elusive.
Evening is reduced to a pause moving past, a fibrous border
that you caress with one finger on the windshield, damp at the
end.
The finger is the part that can feel mist.
And mist, like transparent fabric, hides the two tempos,
the definitive texture from which reality is made,
its length of cloth.

Laguna de los nenúfares

para Virginia

Ella no abrió sus cartas: "no, no, por favor…"
Tiró el filo de la navaja
y no abrió su vena deforme todavía. Aún no.
La bata rosa de tela barata por cortina
le quitaba la visibilidad sostenida con tanto esfuerzo.
Todo tendría al fin que concluir.
Pero cuándo? Cómo?
Una verdad que sólo conoce la liebre que se hunde
en el pantano, tan remota y efímera.
Concluir, empezar, a una distancia prudente de las estatuas
legítimas,
de un tirón o al revés,
tan absurda a la caída contra el cielo.

Sea la memoria de una voz
el sonido de los boliches al caer, golpeándonos,
brillantes, redondos o en semicírculos,
como su impaciencia de caer contra la ventana.
La mirada hacia el atardecer distante
de aquel otro día en que ella vio el puente,
y en el puente abajo, un río,
y dentro de su pequeño bolsillo las piedras
—los boliches— que sonaban con suspicaz indiferencia.
Ellos sabían de tan cerca la mentira, la verdad,
el propósito rojo amarillo, así de redondo, fofo.
Ellos sabían que estaban obligados
a caer, a golpear siempre, y la duración
del tiempo que costaba prepararse para el reencuentro
con el golpe fatal sobre la saya.

Lily pond

for Virginia

She wouldn't open her letters: "No, no, please…"
She threw the razor blade down
and didn't cut her swollen vein. Not yet.
The pink dressing gown made from cheap curtain fabric
took the visibility she sustained with so much work.
In the end, everything would have to arrive at its conclusion.
But when? How?
A truth known only by a hare as it sinks
into a swamp, remote and ephemeral.
Concluding and beginning at a prudent distance from those
legitimated statues,
all in one shot or all backwards,
totally absurd: falling into the sky.

The memory of a voice may be
the noise from jacks falling, hitting us,
shiny, or piled up or in semicircles,
like her impatient fall into the window.
Her gaze toward that other sun setting far away
when she saw the bridge,
and below it a river,
and inside her little pocket, stones
—the jacks—that cracked with a suspicious indifference.
They were so familiar with the lie, with the truth:
a yellow-red target, something rounded like a target, squishy.
They knew they were required
to fall, would always land hard, knew the amount
of time it took to prepare for the reencounter
in the fatal crash, inside her pockets.

Un puente que fue un sitio para estar (aparentemente)
seguros se convirtió en tabla frágil
de indecisión.

Ahora el espejo te devuelve incólume.
Quién eres? Quién eres? Dónde ha quedado la duda?
Allá, bajo el puente, su costado refractado mil veces
por un dolor de lugar que azora todavía
quieto.
Al llegar hay un cerco, es la neblina.
Y la neblina provoca aún más indecisión.
Tenía el panorama, de pronto lo contemplaría de nuevo
por última vez.
Aunque quisiera acercar la mano, tocar,
aquella cabeza que era la suya
sostenida por encima del hombro y la niebla
la traicionaba.

"Siempre era mi hermano…, mi hermano quién salía de las
profundidades de la laguna de los nenúfares" —diría ella
antes de bajar.

A bridge that was a place for keeping (apparently)
safe turned into a plank fragile
with indecision.

Now the mirror returns you unscathed.
Who are you? Who are you? Where has the doubt gone?
There below the bridge, her side refracted a thousand times
through the sorrows of a place
of panic within stillness.
When you arrive there's a fence: the fog.
And the fog provokes still more indecision.
I saw the panorama, would suddenly contemplate it
for the last time.
Though I'd like to reach out, touch her,
the head that used to be hers
drooping on one shoulder and the fog
would betray her.

"It was always my brother… my brother who was emerging from
the depths of the lily pond," she would say
just before she sank.

THE BOOK OF CLIENTS
EL LIBRO DE LAS CLIENTAS
(2005)

Hilos

…llenas de hilos como el
corazón de un avaro…

V. WOOLF

Hilos que se revientan, devaneos.
El cielo es una tela ingrata y las nubes hacen pinzas
sobre el algodón.
"Así lo veo, así."
Arruga un poquito más el entrecejo para ver la maldad
que asoma por el color tisú.
Luego aquel otro (mustio)
hasta taparte con su tono, los pies acurrucados
junto a un marco podrido.
No quiero ver los pies, ¡mis bellos pies!,
bajo pisacosturas mordiendo
una tarde de ¡cuán bella fui! sentada en sus rodillas
suspirando.

Threads

...stringy as a
miser's heart...
V. WOOLF

Threads that are worn through, idle affairs.
The sky is an ungrateful fabric and clouds make darts
in the cotton.
"That's how I see it, that's how."
She wrinkles her forehead a little more to see evil
showing through the tissue's color.
Then that other (gloomy) sky,
until it covers your curled feet in its tone
alongside a rotted frame.
I don't want to see the feet, my beautiful feet!,
under the guide of the needle biting out
an afternoon of how beautiful I was! seated on her knees,
sighing.

Hilos contados

"Tengo los hilos dirigidos hacia abajo (afiladitos)
en pendiente. Algunos
desflecados hacia el borde ..."
—decía mi abuela cuando, encorvada y ciega en su sillón,
arrancaba con las uñas, uno a uno,
aquellos hilos de su dobladillo.
"Cuento los hilos, como días, así que ahorita
estará todo el fleco completo
y ya no me quedará ninguno."
Para ella, los días quedaban detenidos mientras no los tocara.

Hilo de dios, del diablo o la desesperación
pasaban en fila también las carretas (sus bueyes)
"y depositaban unas cajas atadas con cordeles que contenían,
supongo, toda la ropa de alguna familia
que buscaba fortuna o refugio ..."
Así, vi a mi abuela desflecar su pasado en la saya.
La saya de una tela burda gris
y el blanco camisón bordado.
Debajo, nada.
El sillón de orejeras al lado del espejo
y el pedestal de mármol que aún la sostenía.

Ella bajaba la mano del pedestal
y estiraba el festón hasta arrancar otro día, al dolor.
Las cajas quedaban en la esquina contraria,
amontándose.
Refugio sin fortuna y manchas
—que en las manos de mi abuela sobrevivían
a la traición, a las pérdidas.
Ni siquiera temblaba cuando sus hilos en cruz

Counted threads

"I have threads oriented from top to bottom (thin ones),
at a slant. Some of them
are pulling out…"
my grandmother would say, stooped and sightless in her rocker,
as she tore them out of the fringe
with her fingernails, one by one.
"I count the threads like days so now
the entire border will be complete,
no more of them left for me."
For her, days slowed toward stasis when she wasn't fingering
                                                                them.

Thread of divinity, devil or desperation
passing also in a row were carts (their oxen)
"and they set down some boxes tied with cords that held
I suppose all the clothes from some family
out searching for luck or shelter…"
This is how I saw my grandmother fray her past in her skirt.
The skirt of a coarse gray cloth
and the white nightdress, embroidered.
Underneath them, nothing.
The Carmelite chair with great wings next to the mirror
and the marble pedestal that still supported her.

She would lower her hand from the pedestal
and stretch the scalloped trim to pull another day from the pain.
The boxes remained in the opposite corner,
piling up.
Shelter without luck or stains,
which between my grandmother's hands survived
the betrayal, the losses.
She didn't even shudder when her cross of threads

quedaban errantes por unos segundos (o mal torcidos)
la desobedecían por un rato
y el pánico en nosotros arreciaba.
Gracias a su paciencia en "deshilachar" —nos precisaba ella—,
en sacar unos cuantos puntos ganados o perdidos
a la comisura de una tela podrida,
aguantamos el fleco.

wandered off for a few seconds (or twisted),
disobeyed her briefly,
our panic intensifying.
Thanks to her patience—in what she called "unraveling"—
in removing some however many stitches gained or lost
at the corner of a deteriorating fabric,
we endure its edge.

Ámbar

para Osvaldo

Pulso de cuadradas piedras que se caen sostenidas.
Por cada una se desprende
el valor de nuestra amistad.
Cuadrada ciudad como cuentas de muchos colores:
cuadrilátero infernal de cerro en cerro
desordenado para llegar hasta ti.
Cómo cuento estas cuentas tan dispersas?

El vendedor las pesó bien en la pesita sin pasión,
pero lo engañaron.
Despilfarro de cuentas ámbar contra el tiempo
que duró nuestro encuentro.
El resultado de conversar sin aire en la colina
genera una inquietud de contemplar tu mano
(ancha y cortante contra el filo del vaso de cerveza).

Qué ha quedado de nosotros?
La vanidad de mover las piedras
en el aire insatisfecho y sin ilusión?
Hojuelas de maíz tierno contaminadas por el vapor
del distrito, ya quemadas?
Carne cruda de Japón, carne hambrienta
que estremece y entumece la doblez de mi lengua?

Pruebo helado de té verde, "como masticar un jade" —dices,
paralizando mi risa nerviosa al remover con la cucharita de plata
el temblor de la tierra,
ese temblor de mi boca que recibe de tu mano, la joya invisible,
la promesa sostenida que me das de probar,

Amber

for Osvaldo

Bracelet of squares, stones falling in suspension.
The value of our friendship
drops with each one.
City squared like multicolored beads:
hellish quadrilateral, ridge after ridge
displaced to get to you.
How do I account for these counters, so dispersed?

The salesman weighed them with care and without emotion,
but they fooled him.
Spill of amber beads counters the amount of time
our encounter lasted.
The outcome of our airless conversation on the hill
disquiets me, contemplating your hand
(broad and cutting at the edge of your beer glass).

What is left of us?
The vanity of moving stones
through dissatisfied and disillusioned air?
Kernels of fresh corn already contaminated with the steam
from that district, and scorched?
Raw meat from Japan, famished flesh
that agitates and numbs my folded tongue?

I sample green tea ice cream, "like chewing jade," you say,
freezing my nervous titter, using a silver spoon
to take the tremor out of the earth,
the tremor of my mouth receiving the invisible jewel from your
                                                          hand,
the promise you hold up for me to savor,

con la hilaridad de un pasado vencido por el presente otra vez.
"Él fue mi juventud", repito,
y la cuchara suena.
Un broche de plata en la muñeca para cerrar un pacto
con el esfuerzo carbonizado de querer.

Pero las piedras dicen que volverás al comienzo
(tú, conmigo).
Ellas regresan ahora como un pulso finito,
luego volverán como una soga alrededor del cuello
o dentro de un reloj acostumbrado a mentir.
Infinita caravana de piedras sin contar
rodeándonos.
De dos en dos, de tres en tres…
Cuadriláteros portátiles
escupiendo cenizas art decó.

—El pulso por la vida— ha dicho el vendedor siempre estafándonos.
Uno más de aquellos viejos anticuarios
a quien entregamos de por vida el valor de nuestra amistad,
(ámbar prieto) para no adquirir más que la prohibición.

Y lo traje de vuelta, lo escondí bajo la almohada.
Lo oculté como pude para no masticar las veinticuatro horas
cenizas de ámbar.
Porque ya te he perdido muchas veces
entre el rojo solitario del volcán
eructando su roca más incandescente, tú.

Ahora, las piedras que me diste coronarán esta erupción.
Quizás la última erupción bajo mi cabeza
fríamente.

with the hilarity of a past crushed by the present yet again.
"He was my youth," I repeat,
and the spoon clinks.
A silver clasp at the wrist, to seal a pact
with the carbonized exertions of desire.

But the stones say that you will return to the beginning
(you, along with me).
The stones return now as a pulse that is finite,
they'll return later as a rope around your neck
or inside a watch that consistently lies about time.
Infinite caravan of stones countlessly
encircling us.
Two by two, three by three...
Portable quadrilaterals
spitting art deco ashes.

"The pulse for life," says the salesman, continuously conning us.
One more of those old antique dealers
to whom we hand the lifelong value of our friendship
(dark amber), receiving nothing more than prohibition in return.

And I brought it back, hid it under my pillow.
I concealed it as best I could, to keep from chewing amber ashes
twenty-four hours a day.
Because I've already lost you many times
in the crimson solitude of the volcano
expelling its most incandescent chunk of rock: you.

Now the stones you gave me will crown this eruption.
Maybe the last eruption, under my head,
icily.

Las brutas

Cuatro mujeres se ahorcaron en el altiplano
degollaron con paciencia a sus animales
sus veinte cabras
sus dos perros de raza
y los cuerpos
colgaron al vacío.
Pero el vacío tenía una luz morada ese día
y había pájaros presenciando el desangramiento
de aquella sangre joven.
Eran hermanas
y los perros eran amantes
y las cabras pastaban sobre la misma colina
descruzaban sus patas delanteras
con un lento movimiento de felicidad.
Al levantarse, uno no estaba con ánimo de asistir al paisaje.
Uno no oyó el canto de las cabras
al concluir su camino.
Uno no oyó ladrar a los perros
(su silencio es la muerte)
y no hay que volver los ojos
sobre las cumbres nevadas
con las cuatro mujeres colgantes
(pueden ser de arcilla a esta distancia)
figuras de paja seca al sol
espantapájaros
alguna ilusión de ceniza en lo alto.
Detrás, sigue pasando el río
cada vez más claro, más manso.
El viento a cada rato, lo mece.
Nadie se atreve todavía a descolgarlas.
Nadie quiere concebir aquel aullido sin eco.
Mujeres sin hombres (bestias) con las rodillas flacas

Ignorant women

Four women hanged themselves on a high plateau
they cut the throats of their animals with patience
their twenty goats
their two pedigreed dogs
and the bodies dangled
in empty space.
But the space held a purple light that day
and birds were witness to exsanguinations
of that youthful blood.
They were sisters,
the dogs were in love,
the goats grazed on the same hill,
uncrossed their front legs
in slow movements of happiness.
Waking up, one was not in a mood to handle that landscape.
One did not hear the song of goats
completing their walk.
One didn't hear dogs barking
(their silence is death)
and doesn't have to turn and look
across the snowy peaks
with four dangling women
(as if molded from clay, from this distance)
figures of sun-dried straw
scarecrows
some illusion of ashes in the air.
In the background the river keeps moving past
ever more clear, more peaceful.
Pushed by an occasional gust.
No one has dared take them down yet.
No one wants to imagine that echoless howling.
Women without men (beasts) with skinny knees

—no fueron ellas las del grito, las de la queja—
fue más bien de los animales, la lamentación.
Suena un cuerno de caza medieval.
El hombre en una niebla de pasión, recuerdos
y amargura
(baja)
pero ha llegado tarde a rescatarlas.
Luciana se casaba la próxima semana.
No pudo aplazar la decisión colectiva
el rito de morir, de sus hermanas.
Justa zurcía para un orfelinato
y Quisque daba de comer a los animales.
Una vida sencilla, llevaban.
Quisque, Justa, Lucía y Luciana
reventaron el cordel que juntas las ató.
"Las brutas"—les decían.
"Las sabias"—murmuraban.
Contradicción de la representación.
Formalidades.
Cuatro figuras, veinte cabras
y dos perros de raza
caen como semillas en la escarcha.
Una mano, el lomo de un perro, la falange
un cuello largo cortado en cruz
su hocico (el tuyo).
El cordel que las funde es el límite?
El límite fue ese grito que nunca se escuchó?
Cómo apartar los ojos de un paisaje
sin perros ni cabras?

—the ones crying out were not women, the ones whining—
lamentation came from the animals.
Blowing of a medieval hunting horn.
The man in a cloud of passion, memories
and bitterness
(lowering)
but he came too late to save them.
Luciana was to be married the following week.
She couldn't stave off the collective decision,
the rite of death decided by her sisters.
Justa did mending for an orphanage
and Quisque fed the animals.
A simple life, the one they led.
Quisque, Justa, Lucía and Luciana
split the cord that knotted them together.
"Ignorant women," people called them.
"Wise women," they muttered.
Contradictory representation.
Formalities.
Four figures, twenty goats
and two pedigreed dogs
fall like seeds in frost.
A hand, a dog's back, phalange
a long neck cut in four parts
its muzzle (yours).
Cord where they fade into each other: the limit?
Was limitation the cry no one ever heard?
How do you pull your eyes away from a landscape
without dogs or goats?

Neblina en la capital

Traición del hilo que aparece
y desaparece
cuando el discípulo está preparado para partir.
Es esa neblina de hoy que vemos arder
sobre la ciudad.
Neblina de cal, polvorosa,
que te hará encontrar (en su propio día)
la fe.
Una cantidad de hojas suficientes para secar al mar
de la bahía morada.
Cuánto tiempo contemplé la raya divisoria
entre la rama y el agua.
Tantas como caí, caí
en los círculos viciosos
de mentir.
"Errar, errar" —decían siempre los círculos
y el hilo se partía.
Esto se llama merma, comprendí.
La rama prieta entró por fin al agua
y tropezó con la neblina de hoy (dorándose)
para que comprendiera la cantidad de fe necesaria
que rebasará este día, y aquel
con su suave movimiento ondulado.
Porque es el cielo quien abre la puerta
y su color nos descansa la ira,
la ansiedad.
Después, aparta los misterios, los hábitos
—ese crujir miserable detrás de una neblina que se va
cuando aparece (otra cortina más espesa)
¿el alma?

Mist in the capital city

Betrayal of the thread that appears
and disappears
when the disciple is prepared to set out.
Today that's the mist we see burning
over the city.
Mist of lime, powdery,
(on its own day) it will lead you to find
faith.
A sufficient quantity of leaves to dry in seawater
from the purple bay.
How long did I contemplate the line dividing
the branch from the water.
So many times that I fell, fell again
into vicious circles
speaking lies.
"To err, to err," the circles always said
and the thread pulled apart.
I realized: this is called wastage.
Finally the dark branch dipped into water
colliding with today's mist (putting on its gold)
so I would understand the necessary amount of faith
which this day will exceed, and that day
with its gentle undulating motion.
Because it's the sky who opens the door
and its color rests ire upon us,
anxiety.
Afterwards it separates mysteries, customs
—the wretched creaking behind a mist that goes away
when it appears (another thicker screen),
the soul?

Céline y las mujeres

Soy el hijo de una zurcidora de puntillas antiguas
—decía Céline, reclamando un espacio—
y por eso conozco las delicadezas del infierno.
Soy uno de esos pocos hombres que sabe diferenciar
la batista de los encajes de Valenciennes de los de Brujas...
Hasta cortarlos sé.
Con una tijera de mango rojo he cortado la sangre.
Y toda la ceremonia del amor no era más
que un coágulo.
Una mancha caliente.

Por eso, tengo a mi cargo la puntilla del tiempo,
esa que pende de los finales
y los remates bien estirados.
Y no hay nada más relacionado con el estilo,
que un tejido de encaje en la sábana —eso lo apunta hacia ella—
cuando vuelve de esconder el supuesto cesto de la costura
de los ojos de él.

Hay una vela derritiéndose a mi lado,
una llama que no se volverá a encender.
Es la llama de mi madre, y con ella,
toda mi vida desciende.
Cuánto esperma regado por el plato, sobre el mantel,
entre la sábana de anoche.

Ese es su triunfo: caer, decaer.
Cada mancha en los brazos
—pobre sabiduría de marcar
los espacios (la enormidad)
de esas zonas pegajosas,
embadurnadas de pasado y desconfianza.

Céline and the women

I'm the son of a mother who mends antique lace edging
—Céline used to say, claiming a space—
and that's why I know the intricacies of hell.
I'm one of few men who can differentiate
batiste in Valenciennes lacework from the one used in Bruges...
I even know how to cut them.
With mango-red scissors I've cut off blood flow.
And the whole ceremony of love was only
a clot.
A warm stain.

That's why I have in my care the edging of time.
Hanging from its borders,
double stitches nicely smoothed.
And there's nothing else involved in style,
just lace texture on a sheet—pointing it at her—
when she comes back from hiding the supposed sewing basket
from his eyes.

There's a candle melting next to me,
a flame that won't be lit again.
My mother's flame, and with it
my entire life descends.
A quantity of candlewax spilling on the plate, over the tablecloth,
into last night's bedsheet.

That's its victory: falling, waning.
Each spot on her arms
—poor wisdom of marking
spaces (enormity)
those sticky zones
smeared with past and distrust.

Son cosas de los dos.
Mi madre y él tejían a propósito de una destrucción
seguida de otra, con ahínco.

Cansado de ser un gozador
(y ella de ser una zurcidora)
se acuesta sobre su regazo.
Criatura de esperma que se va derritiendo
en sílabas primero —supongo que será el origen—,
sin demostraciones, después.
Balbucea el remate, la cicatrización.
Ella es más hombre, él más mujer.
Así se han comprendido provocando un corte, un estilo.
La palabra que encuentran en el semen
de-rre-ti-do
dice "unificar".
Luego, "poseer".

Él la sigue mirando por el hueco sin rematar.
Ella oprime la mano que tiembla, pero no afloja
la puntada.
Saldrá una letra, un coágulo de nata
de insoportable olor
que también se agrietará.
Por más que pretendieran armar este tejido juntos, se zafa.
—Es la familia, Céline, la voz de trueno de mi padre
quien no me dejará torcer la palabra final
con ese hilo tan blando
que va quedando rezagado,
pero que sube al fin por la frágil esquina del paño,
y dice: "traición."

No me quejo, la veo bien, casi la toco,
a distancia.

These are their things.
He and my mother deliberately spinning one destruction
after another, diligently.

Tired of being fun-loving
(and she of mending lace)
the writer, or is it my father, falls asleep in her lap.
Candle creature who melts
first into syllables—origin, I suppose—
without any proofs afterwards.
The final touch stammers, scar tissue.
She is more man, he more woman.
They've understood each other this way, provoking a cut, a style.
The word they find in the semen,
li-que-fy-ing,
says "unite."
Then, "possess."

He goes on looking at the word through a hole, without finishing.
She presses the trembling hand but doesn't slow
her stitch.
A letter will emerge, a clot of cream
with an unbearable odor;
it will crack too.
The more they work together to assemble this fabric, the more it
                                                    pulls apart.
"It's the family, Céline": thundering voice from my father
who won't let me twist the final word
in a soft thread
continually pulling apart,
though in the end it climbs the delicate corner of the kerchief
to say "betrayal."

I'm not complaining, I can see it very well, can almost touch it,
from far away.

Antes de que la vela y mi rostro
dentro del tuyo
se apaguen.

Before the candle and my face
inside yours
blow out.

BLACK FOREST
BOSQUE NEGRO
(2005)

Deja ver si vino...

Deja ver si vino la libreta verde jaspeado musgo
con tapa de cartón,
algo donde espiar la algarabía del otro.

Dime Ismael, ¿por qué estoy triste?

Perdí los espejuelos pecosos,
perdí la esquina de San Rafael
tu mano parda.

Estoy en el lado este de las cosas
donde no hay metafísica o rumor
que apañe al gong que llama.
Una sombra entra al comedor
otra sale de mí.
El perro-monstruo alucinante
me apresa en su mordida sin rabia.
Depositada entre piel y diente
la saliva viscosa del mundo
me embarra la boca amarga del desinterés.

Dime Ismael, ¿por qué estoy triste?

Deja ver si vino la libreta verde,
tal vez me salve de la inmediatez
que al fin, me espanta.
La libreta verde de sobrevivir la ridícula
escasez de vivir.

¿A quién llamar Ismael
en estas "vacaciones del mundo"
lejana a todo lo que sea

See if it arrived...

See if the moss-green notebook arrived, the one
with a marbled cardboard cover,
a place for someone else's gibberish.

Tell me, Ismael, why am I sad?

I lost my speckled hand mirrors,
lost the corner of San Rafael,
your brown hand.

I'm on this side of things
where there's no metaphysics or rumor
to manage sound coming from the gong.
One shadow enters the dining room
another leaves me.
The incredible dog-monster
catches me in its jaw without fury.
Settled between skin and tooth
coated with the world's sticky saliva
from the sour mouth of unselfishness.

Tell me, Ismael, why am I sad?

Tell me if the green notebook came,
maybe it can save me from immediacy
which, after all, is terrifying.
The green notebook for surviving the ridiculous
scarcity of existence.

Ismael, whom do I call
on these "vacations from the world,"
distant from anything forming

un círculo perpetuo e
imposible?

II

El poema se me pierde
el poema se disloca.
Estoy seca.
(Los exfoliantes de vivir me han secado.)
"Cremas para piel seca" venden ahí.
La vagina seca arde.
La palabra seca y lúcida arde. Relumbra mate.
¿Cómo desmontar al personaje del carrusel,
su impaciencia de proclamar cada ardid?
¿Cómo desmontar la palabra que se agarra y se sujeta
sin un fin, la palabra no dicha,
la ardilla que se esconde de mis ojos
y escapa?

La niña busca dentro de la maleta
una libreta verde, la subasta de un porvenir
que ya es pasado.
La plastilina para modelar las cosas
del entretiempo.

El mundo está de vacaciones en el mundo, Ismael.
Sale un poema portátil.
O ni siquiera sale.

a perpetual or impossible
circle?

II

My poem gets lost
my poem dislocates.
I am dry.
(The exfoliants of existence dried me out.)
They sell "lotions for dry skin" there.
My dry vagina is burning.
My dry, lucid word is burning. A gleaming matte.
How do I dismantle my carousel character,
her impatient heralding of every ruse?
How do I dismantle the word, which clings and adheres
endlessly, the unsaid word,
a squirrel who dodges my sight
and gets away?

The girl rifles through the suitcase
for a green notebook, the bid for a future
already past.
Plasticine for modeling things
of a changing era.

The world is on vacation in the world, Ismael.
A portable poem is what comes out.
Or doesn't.

Bosque negro

"...Él querría dulces. Pregúntale..."

J.M.

No se preocupe.
No nos vamos a robar los dulces
Ya las moscas han entrado a la vitrina.
El señor dice… "dulce de moscas" y corriendo,
a pesar del cansancio
lo vamos a probar.
Desde las horas en que el dulce llegó
ha pasado la vida (la eternidad),
todo el ridículo tiempo
acumulado por la espera.
El dulce llega con una postergación suficiente
para ser dañino.

Caja cerrada: mi inspiración
como la mosca atraviesa el cristal.
Nieve de nata podrida es la cubierta.
Mojo los dedos, los enchumbo y pruebo
con la cara de esa niña
que esperaba relámpagos de Navidad.
Pero la mosca observó el veneno dormido
en la masa contrahecha.
"El horno es chico, no cabe aún mi cabeza" —resoplo,
y la mosca se percata de que tengo desajustes
(arritmia)
parálisis de la intensidad.

El dulce quema la garganta,
"¡no me vendan algo podrido!" —grito.
La cafetería norte al Parque Central va a cerrar

Black Forest

"He'll want candy. Ask him…"

J.M.

Don't worry.
We're not going to steal the candy.
Flies already got in the shop window.
The man says… "fly candy" and
in spite of our exhaustion,
we'll come running to taste it.
In the hours since the candy arrived
life has passed by, eternity,
all the ridiculous time
accumulating as we waited.
The candy arrives with a delay sufficient
to be dangerous.

Closed box: my inspiration,
like the fly, walks across the glass.
Spoiled cream snow on top.
I moisten my fingers, wiggle them, and sample the frosting
with the face of a girl
expecting lightning on Christmas.
But the fly sensed venom dormant
in the misshapen lump.
"The oven is small, my head doesn't even fit inside," I sigh,
and the fly notices that I have disorders in my sensations,
paralysis of my intensity
(arrhythmia).

The candy burns my throat,
I shout, "Don't you sell me something spoiled!"
The café north of Central Park will close,

179

su techo rosa viejo oscurecido.
Tengo sueños con dulces y enemigos.
Pruebo la crema reluciente
a esa hora puntual de la locura
y un sabor ocre atraganta mi imposibilidad.

La mosca sale y vuelve, ella sabe bien
que nunca se sale sino que se vuelve
a la vitrina.

its rose-pink ceiling old, darkened.
I dream of candy and enemies.
I taste the sparkling cream
at that punctual hour of insanity
and the taste of ochre chokes my incapacity.

The fly goes away and it comes back. It knows well
that you can't go away without coming back
to the shop window.

Reparaciones

Mi reparación tiene que ser total, no parcial. Como la ciudad después de un aguacero. He sido devastada. La dentadura entera, el corazón, las glándulas. Buscar al carpintero, al decorador, al plomero que coloque los tanques. A la gente, gente, gente que coloque la respiración artificial.

Reparations

My reparation must be total, not partial. Like the city after a torrential rain. I have been devastated. The full set of teeth, the heart, the glands. Find the carpenter, the decorator, the plumber to set up water tanks. And the people, people, people to set up artificial respiration.

Aceites

Aceite de cocina sin colesterol, aceite de hígado de bacalao, aceite de oliva...

Uno me servía para obtener largas pestañas, otro para engordar en el extremo de la delgadez. Aceites para encender las ilusiones y pedir a los santos. ¡Cuántas velas de algodón quemadas en mi velatorio de creer! Empiezo a cocinar otra vez la comida del desprendimiento. Aceite prieto, mugriento de todos los días, en una cazuela cuyo humo es el final de todo lo que fui. Azabaches. Grasas inertes, insensatas. Grasas ligeras que me queman la sangre y el dolor (colesterol). Ahora preparo aceite con ajo para llevárselo a mi hijo en la prisión. Botella plástica para sobrevivir sin perder la combustión. Antes pensé en la metafísica, ahora soy realista. El aceite es el combustible de la desesperación. El aceite engrasa y mata los deseos del "yo". Un aceite que nunca tuve, aquel de la lubricación artificial. También lo vi en aquella tienda de Miami Beach y dije que lo compraría, pero al final tuve miedo a pronunciar su nombre.

Oils

Cholesterol-free cooking oil, cod-liver oil, olive oil...
One served to bring me long eyelashes, another to fatten my extreme slenderness. Oils to light illusions and petition the saints. So many cotton balls dotted with oil, burned as candles at the wake I hold over belief! I go back to cooking detachment foods. Dark oil, filthy from everyday use, in a broth whose vapors are remains of everything I was before. Jet blacks. Inert and unwise fats. Lighter fats that burn my blood and pain (cholesterol). Now I infuse oil with garlic to take to my son in prison. A plastic bottle to survive without loss of combustibility. Before I thought about metaphysics; now I'm a realist. Oil is the combustible for desperation. Oil fattens and kills the self's desires. An oil I never got—the one for artificial lubrication. I saw it too in a store in Miami Beach, and I said I would buy it, but in the end I was afraid to say its name.

Tomates "Del Monte"

Tomate maduro de las ensaladas. Del pan de las tardes antes de ir a la universidad cuando solía visitar a mi novio de Nuevo Vedado. Ese tomate me llenaba el espíritu. Podía comer pan con tomate y salían enrojecidas las metáforas. (No me gusta el verde, dicen que es cancerígeno). Comía mi pan con tomate y oía a Wagner. El cartón preservado del tomate, Tannhäuser, y su corazón jadeaba. El músculo era largo como la tarde de verano cuya luz entraba por la avenida 26. Ahora no soporto su acidez Tropical Island: ese cartón preservado del tomate sin oír a Wagner.

Del Monte Tomatoes

Ripe salad tomato. With my afternoon toast before college classes, when I used to visit my boyfriend in Nuevo Vedado. That tomato satisfied my spirit. I could eat bread and tomato, and the metaphors came out flushed with red. (I don't like green tomato; it's said to be a carcinogen.) I'd eat my bread and tomato and listen to Wagner. The carton saved from the tomato, Tannhäuser, and his heart would gasp. Its muscle was long as the summer afternoon whose light entered from 26th Avenue. Now I can't stand its Tropical Island acidity: that carton saved from the tomato, minus listening to Wagner.

Detergente

He lavado los pisos, la memoria, su obsesión...

Detergent

I've washed down floors, memory, the obsession...

Comida para gatos o la cantidad hechizada

Los gatos son los más engañados con esta cuestión de la escasez. Les echo pedacitos de carne, pedacitos de pescados, pedacitos de cualquier cosa. Nunca cosas completas. Ellos suspiran por lo que vendrá. Me miran, tienen la ilusión de que vendrá después, "La cantidad", por eso resisten. La cantidad es para ellos, el sueño.

Cat food, or, the great captivating quantity

My cats are the most deceived about this situation of scarcity. I throw them tiny bits of meat, tiny bits of fish, tiny bits of whatever. Never entire things. They sigh over what is yet to come. They gaze at me, they have the illusion that "the Great Quantity" will come later, that's why they hold out. The great quantity is, for them, the dream.

Voces

Llamar a... *mandy, falcón, osvaldo, ponte, richard, a cuál, dónde están, qué número, a ninguno. No hay nadie. Sale la grabadora imitando una voz, mintiendo una voz. Ya me acostumbraré, ya me acostumbré. "Cuca-la-macara-títere fue..." También he puesto una que lentamente codifica mi voz. No tengo voz. Es final de siglo, final de un quejido, estertor. (Recuerdo, "Compañía" de Beckett, lo que puede una voz). El texto para lograr la voz. Su lenguaje que obedece a ella. Te llamo para recordar el sabor de tu voz, el sin sonido de tu voz. No te da ningún placer oír la mía —me dices, lloro y cuelgo. Mi voz no tiene estilo. Es ronca, áspera, infantil. Ni siquiera hallo modulación en mi voz. La voz del otro lado me falta. No obstante, insisto.*

Busco en la agenda (una para el país, otra para el extranjero).

La de afuera, se va llenando la de afuera...

No queda nadie aquí, no queda nadie. Un eco en el desierto. El lóbulo lleno de arena, ventisca, rumor...

¿Hubo alguien alguna vez con esa misma voz?

Debo estar confundiendo los tonos de discar.

Voices

Calling... mandy, falcón, osvaldo, ponte, richard, which one, where are they, at what number, none of them. No one's there. The answering machine goes off in imitation of a voice, falsifying a voice. I'll get used to it, already got used to it. "Eeny meeny miney mo..." I've set up a machine too that slowly codifies my voice. I have no voice. It's the end of a century, the end of a moan, death rattle. (I recall Beckett's *Company*, what a voice can do.) The text to achieve a voice. Language that obeys it. I call you up to remember the taste of your voice, the soundlessness of your voice. It gives you no pleasure to hear mine, you say. I cry and hang up. My voice has no style. It's gravelly, harsh, childlike. Not even any modulation in it. The voice on the other end is missing. I persist anyway.

I page through the address book (one for this country, another for outside it).

The one for outside, it's filling up, the one for outside...

No one is left here, no one. An echo in the desert. Lobe full of sand, snowstorm, mumbling...

Was there once someone who had that exact voice?

I must be getting dial tones confused.

Fricandel

Busco como si fueran joyas,
como si fueran amuletos o ilusiones...
los mandados, las palabras.
Me esclavizan y doblegan.
Granos
Vegetales
Leche
Huevos
Pescado
¿Carnes?
No había hígado ni pollo.
Sólo, pasta de oca
corazón de pollo
molleja (pescuezo)
perro sin tripa
corazón extendido
y doliente.

Cuando llegó Almelio con la noticia que le dio su madre:
—Y ¿dónde consiguió ese bistec? —le pregunto, ilusionada.
Pues, en la toronja —me responde con sonrisa infantil—,
entre la masa acolchada de la toronja.
En el torrente esponjoso de la fruta más ácida,
con la corteza de desear
algo caliente.
"Se adoba y queda igualitico" —dice el poeta y guarda su toronja,
confiado.

¡Bistec de toronja! —exclamo.
¿Poema de papa? —pienso.

Fricandeau

I go after them as though they were jewels,
were amulets or illusions...
the errands, the words.
They enslave me. They humble me.
Grains
Vegetables
Milk
Eggs
Fish
Meats?
No liver or chicken.
Just goose paste
chicken heart
gizzard (neck)
stomachless dog
stretched and
painful heart.

When Almelio arrived with news from his mother
I asked, hopeful, Where did you get that beefsteak?
Well, from grapefruit, he answered with a childish smile,
from the quilted mass of fruit.
In the spongy torrent of the most acidic fruit,
with the rind from desiring
something hot.
"Pickle it, it's just like beef," says the poet, and he guards his
                                                    grapefruit,
trusting.

"Beef from grapefruit!" I exclaim.
"Poem from potato?" I wonder.

ACKNOWLEDGMENTS

Kristin Dykstra's English translations were supported in part by a grant from the National Endowment for the Arts. To find out more about how National Endowment for the Arts grants impact individuals and communities, visit www.arts.gov.

NATIONAL ENDOWMENT for the **ARTS**
arts.gov

The following translations from this manuscript were published by magazines and organizations, often in earlier renditions. In some cases, Rodríguez went on to edit her Spanish originals as well. We greatly appreciate the support from the editors throughout all stages of this process.

- "I don't hear, don't hear Bach anywhere...": *Review: Literature and Arts of the Americas.*
- Reina María Rodríguez, *Catch and Release*, tr. Kristin Dykstra. Linocuts by Alejandro Sainz (Tuscaloosa & Havana: Parallel Editions, 2014). Bilingual chapbook of seven poems, produced by the University of Alabama Book Arts Program in 2014: this is a collaborative project with the

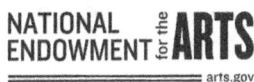

Taller Experimental de Gráfica in Havana, Cuba. A Havana artist created prints that appeared with poems and translations in the chapbooks. The following poems appeared there: "Jigs and lures," "The classroom turtle / La tortuga del aula," "Catch and release," "Fishermen, rough / Pescadores, crudos," "Gyotaku / Giotakus," "Winterbane / Invenio."

- "Fishermen, rough": *The Whole Island* (University of California Press) and NEA Writers' Corner.
- "Breeze over the land," "The Law in Sainte-Victoire": *West Branch*.
- "How it had to be," "The whistle blows," "Orphan's Song": *MAKE: A Chicago Magazine*.
- "The mother, the piano" and "If I'd had": *Bombay Gin*.
- "Gyotaku": *Fascicle*.
- "The word *pitcher*" and "Jigs and lures": *Mandorla: New Writing from the Americas / Nueva escritura de las Américas*.
- "Threads," "Counted threads," and "Mist in the capital city": *Words without Borders*.
- "Ignorant women" and "Céline and the women." *Review: Literature and Art of the Americas*.
- "Undertow": *INTI*.
- "Fishermen, rough," "Black Forest," "Reparations," "Oils," "Del Monte Tomatoes," "Detergent," "Fricandeau," "Cat food, or, the great captivating quantity," and "Voices": *MiPOesias: Revista Literaria*.

INDEX

JIGS AND LURES: SELECTED POEMS | REINA MARÍA RODRÍGUEZ

Made in Miami Beach ~ Printing as needed

◊◊◊

2024

www.ingramcontent.com/pod-product-compliance
Lightning Source LLC
Chambersburg PA
CBHW020155090426
42734CB00008B/831